Art of Growing Money

A COMPLETE GUIDE FOR MUTUAL FUND INVESTMENT

CHHABILESH PATEL

Mutual Fund Distributor

© **Chhabilesh Patel 2022**

All rights reserved

All rights reserved by author. No part of this publication may be reproduced, stored in a retrieval system or transmitted in any form or by any means, electronic, mechanical, photocopying, recording or otherwise, without the prior permission of the author.

Although every precaution has been taken to verify the accuracy of the information contained herein, the author and publisher assume no responsibility for any errors or omissions. No liability is assumed for damages that may result from the use of information contained within.

First Published in May 2022

ISBN: 978-93-5628-102-8

BLUEROSE PUBLISHERS
www.BlueRoseONE.com
info@bluerosepublishers.com
+91 8882 898 898

Cover Design:
Sheetal Netraj Patel
M +91 9179748568
email: sheetalpatidar615@gmail.com

Typographic Design:
Sheetal Netraj Patel

Distributed by: BlueRose, Amazon, Flipkart

SOHAM CAPIGROW

Art of Growing Money

Mutual Fund Investment Guide

Chhabilesh Patel
9638394693
sohamcapigrow@gmail.com

This book will provide many insights to not only those who are just commencingtheir investments but also to them who are investing through Mutual funds for a long period of time. This book will guide all MF investors to reach their financial goals and have a smooth financial journey.

Foreword

Dear Mutual Fund investors,

As we are completing our advisory Journey of 25 Years and celebrating Silver Jubilee, we at Soham Capigrow are proud to present this excellent work done by Chhabilesh Patel.

Prudent CAS has been an integral part of the Mutual Fund distributor's community and part of investors of Mutual Funds in terms of helping, supporting, and educating investors through investor awareness programs. The investor's participation would have not been possible without the effort of many dedicated MFDs across the country. Today it is the need to encourage young investorsto invest through Mutual funds with correct knowledge and education of financial products. It is necessary that everyone should take part in building a strong economy in India.

Mr. Chhabilesh Patel, who joined Prudent Corporate Advisory Services (Prudent CAS) as a Mutual Fund Distributor in the year 2006 makes a cogent and persuasive case as to why the investment through Mutual funds is not only remunerative but also impacts the lifestyle of large society and investors. With more than two and half decades of excellence in the field of the Mutual fund industry, it is agreat pleasure to be a part of dispensing this invaluable book to educate more and more investors.

We are sure this book will provide many insights to not only those who are just new to investment in Mutual funds but also to those who are investing in Mutual funds for a long period of time.

We thank you for your support and wish you will take maximum advantage of the insight provided in this book to reach your financial goals and have a smooth financial journey.

With warm regards,

Prudent Corporate Advisory Services

Disclaimer and risk factors

The information contained in this book is extracted from various public sources and written on the basis of the knowledge and experience of the writer. All reasonable care has been taken at the time of publication. The contains of this book are for the information of the person to whom it is provided without any liability whatsoever on the part of **"Soham Capigrow"** or any associated persons or any employee thereof. We are not soliciting any action based on the material and are for general information only.

Investing in an equity Mutual Fund is risky. Investors should invest based on their risk ability. This book is only for information and should not be considered as investment advice. Neither the author nor greynim information technology would be responsible for any losses incurred based on a decision taken after reading this book.

This book is only for Private Circulation to those who would like to read it.

Mutual Fund Investment is subject to market risk, read all scheme related documents carefully before investing, or contact your Mutual Fund distributor before investing.

Contents

About this book.. viii
Preface... x
How to read this book?... xiii

1. What is saving and investing?................................... 1
2. Know beforeinvesting. 6
3. Know your financial goals. 11
4. What are Mutual Funds?...15
5. Advantages and disadvantages of Mutual Fund. ...36
6. Principles of Mutual Fund Investing.......................43
7. Understanding Risk Factors and market volatility..50
8. Important terms used in Mutual Fund. 59
9. SIP – STP – SWP..67
10. Taxation on Mutual funds: How Mutual Funds taxed?..76
11. Myths and factsabout mutual funds. 84
12. Financial Freedom – Howcan you win it? 90
13. The Role of anadvisor! 111
14. Wealth creation formulas and moments of inspiration..118

About this book

Today people are not much aware of savings and investing. This book will guide people to know all about how to make their money grow through mutual funds and their financial management. Managing finances to meet all future requirements can be a very crucial and complicated task. In schools and colleges, all the subjects are taught and grown- up educated people learn to earn money but they do not learn about how to manage their hard-earned money. Management of money is not being taught in the school and colleges by teachers and professors. This book will teach how to handle and manage money once they start earning money.

People keep making common financial mistakes and take wrong decisions due to lack of financial knowledge, lack of planning, wasteful spending, and so on. This book on Mutual funds will help people to know the importance of investing and how their money can grow to meet their future financial goals.

People have many kinds of myths about investing in mutual funds. So this book will turn their myths into facts when they will read related topics covered in this book. For peopleto know why mutual fund? Because they are professionally managed and easy and efficient to invest in. If you have a desire to be rich and wealthy then this book is for you. If you have big dreams, you think big, and need the courage to achieve your dreams, then this book is surly for you.

All topics of this book have been managed with illustrations, examples and in easy to understand language. There are different mutual funds schemes that you will come to know about, you will learn how to manage risk and return to reach your financial goals.

Happy investing!

Preface

We have been a Mutual Fund distributor for over 25 Years now. I have built my work drop by drop and it had no shortcut. The journey in the last 25 years was not smooth and it will not be smooth even in the future, but I walked and walked solving challenges, educating myself with a hope to serve all the investors came across during my journey so far.

I worked for my investors with a motto that they get financial freedom and beat inflation in their lives.

I was born and brought up in Burhanpur, MP till my graduation. I started my first job in Mumbai as a cashier in a sales and marketing office in June 1978 with Rs.350/- per month. I joined Textile Industry in Mumbai as a trainee in the QC department in 1980 and served the textile industry for 22 years and during this period I visited Saudi Arabia and Turkey.

I made up my mind not to serve for any company and do something on my own, so first I started personal tuitions to primary students. It was a painful period of my life with a long-term vision. Soon I joined LIC of India and in June 2006 I became MF Distributor and joined Prudent CAS (National MF Distributor)

It is my nature to adopt and follow the advice that I recommend to others. So I started first investing in Mutual Funds. Initially, I had no knowledge of Mutual Fund investments.

Mutual fund's awareness was also very less among people. So it was a challenging task for me. I had to make a lot of efforts to educate people about mutual fund investment. For this I started educating myself by taking training, reading books, attending seminars of experts from the MF industry. In the year 2008 when the market corrected by 60%, it was a tough time to handle my few investors who had invested on my advice. I convinced my investors to hold their investment for two years to grow back their hard-earned money.

During my journey to date, I came across many challenges and changes by MF regulator which I handled and played my role consistently. I can say that MF distributors have made a good contribution to the growth of investors along with their growth.

For a long time, I was thinking to write a book like this. My aim to write this book is to educate, provide awareness of Mutual funds among new investors and the young generation so that they make informed decisions and achieve their financial goals and dreams. It is only because of my own experience I got the inspiration from writing this book to add my experience in the form of words, tables, and calculations which can be benefited much larger investors.

Being an MFD, I got the opportunity to interact with many best minds and many new and old investors in Gujarat and neighboring states. This enriched my own learning and I have captured many of them in this book.

Friends and dear investors, my attempt of sharing this book with you is all about what I have learned in the past 25 years and it is a sum-up of my own experience and collection of knowledge. I have only expectation from this book contents that I wish all of you to grow your net worth and achieve what you aspire in life.

I think this book is worth reading and following principlesof investing, please suggest more and more people read it.

Chhabilesh Patel.

Mutual Fund Distributor.

Soham CapiGrow... let your money earn.

How to read this book?

Read this book from beginning to end. Every topic is set in a sequence to provide financial knowledge. Do not read this book as a novel, you may get bored. Do not read it with any pre opinions. Read it at least twice for maximum benefit.

This book will give ideas for mutual fund investment to achieve your dreams and can help you in increasing your wealth. You can choose the idea which will work for you.

This book can be treated as an investment of a few hours, a few days or a few months when you read it, In return, you will surely have some take-away lessons which will be worth your time investment.

If you like this book, please suggest more and more people read it. If you have any suggestions, please do write to us.

Soham Caigrow...

sohamcapigrow@gmail.com

What is saving and investing?

When we use the words saving and Investing, people 90% of them – think it's exactly the same thing. Saving and investing are two important concepts for building a sound financial portfolio for a sound financial life, but both are not the same thing. Both can help achieve a comfortable financial future, you need to know the differences and when it is bestto save and when it is best to invest.

The biggest difference is the level of risk taken. Saving results in you earning a lower return with no risk or very little risk while investing will allow you to earn higher returns with the risk of loss on capital.

When it comes to investing, most of the people say that money is put into share market and it is very risky and we could lose our hard earned money. Some people think putting money in to share market is a gambling with money.

When we ask peoples what is difference between saving and Investment, most of peoples are confused and not able to differentiate correctly. People get mix up both terms saving with investment and investment with saving.

SAVINGS VS. INVESTING

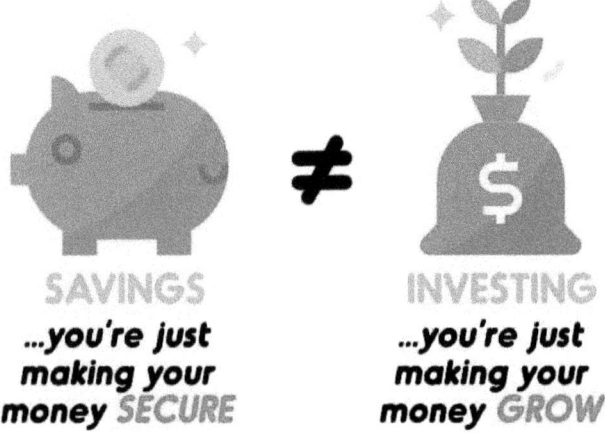

So the first step is to know the differences between saving and investing and why you need both to help build long-term wealth.

Here are the following points which will show the difference between saving and investing.

Saving Vs Investing

When it comes to investing, most of the people say that money is put into share market and it is very risky and we could lose our hard earned money. Some people think putting money in to share market is a gambling with money.

When we ask peoples what is difference between saving and Investment, most of peoples are confused and not able to differentiate correctly. People get mix up both terms saving with investment and investment with saving.

Saving	Investing
It is a Debt. Putting money for future.	It is an Equity. Putting money for future with risk.
It is money landing and borrowing.	It is an ownership of a Business.
Low risky gives low returns.	Low to High risky gives returns as per risk taken.
Good for short term of 1-2 years.	Very good for Long term 5 years & more.
Very risky for long term.	Very risky for short term.
Capital is safe but reduces purchasing power.	Capital is grown & increases purchasing power.
Focus to avoid Capital loss. (Fear)	Focus to grow your Capital. (Confidence)
You work for money. (Aimless)	Money works for you. (Goal Based)
Money do not earn for you.	Money earns money for you
Man at work. (Passive income)	Money at work. (Active Income)
Capital protection tools.	Wealth creation tools.
Game of not to lose.	Game of only to win.
No worries. (Demands nothing)	Need patience. (Demands Planning)

What is saving and investing?

Does not beat inflation.	Beats the inflation.
Returns are paid as per time.	Returns are paid on results.
It is working income. (For Bills & Payments)	It is net worth. (For Dividends & Returns)
Your money is at Job.	Your money is at Business.
Lazy & idle money.	Smart and efficient money.
Easily earned money.(You are controlled by Money)	Hard earned money. (Money controlled by you)
Single digit returns.	Double digit returns.
Traditional way of saving.	Smart way of Investment.
Make you poor & just can survive life. (Enslaves)	Make you wealthy & indulge your life. (Liberates)
Parking place of money.	Manufacturing place of money.
Gain is taxable (TDS) If you save Rs.5000 per month for 20 Years @ 8% will be Rs. 29.64 lakh. Saving Bank a/c, Fixed Deposit, RD, PPF, Post etc.	Gain is Tax efficient. If you invest Rs.5000 per month for 20 years @ 15% will grow to Rs.75.79 lakh. Stocks, Mutual Funds, Bonds, ETFs, Property etc.

Saving Vs Investing

Once you know and understand the terms of saving and investing, you will be able to take the correct decision for deploying your hard-earned money as per your need and financial requirements.

In Mutual Funds, people can invest in Debt as well as in Equity funds. One can invest purely in Debt or purely 100% in

Equity or can invest in a combination of both Debt and Equity. This type of investing decides their risk and return but for equity investing a long horizon of investment is required.

Mutual fund gives all that opportunity to invest as per risk and time horizon.

Since 1996, every year Rs. 1,00,000/- invested in PPF or HDFC Tax Saver Fund, Valuation as on January 01, 2015

Savings (Public Provident Fund - PPF)	Investments (Tax saver fund ELSS)
Total PPF savings : Rs. 19,00,0000/-	Total ELSS savings : Rs. 19,00,0000/-
Valuation : Rs. **46,83,583/-**	Valuation : Rs. **5,53,53,757/-**
CAGR Return : **8.57%**	CAGR Return : **29.44%**

Note: Above comparison is only for understanding.

So which is better? Saving or Investing?

Neither saving or investing is better in all circumstances; the right choice depends on your current financial position. You need to follow two rules:

- If you need money within a year or so or you want to use it as an emergency fund, a saving or FD is best.
- If you do not need money for next 5 years or more and can take risk on capital, then you likely should invest the money.

Know beforeinvesting.

If you are thinking to invest in Mutual funds, you are on the right path because investing through Mutual funds is the besttool for wealth creation over a long period of time. The advantage of investing through mutual funds is that it is a modern tool to be wealthy.

In our day-to-day lives, whenever we decide to make any purchase, say buying a home washing machine, we do detailed research, look at each component, look at prices and then make a decision on which one to buy. This knowledge about what to expect from the product ensures we have a good experience with what we buy. The same is with Mutual Funds. Before investing in them, you need to be aware of a few things that will ensure you have a rewarding investing experience.

We tell you about the 6 things you need to know before investing in Mutual Funds.

1. Different Mutual Fund Categories Have Different Risk Levels

The first and important point is that the risk of every mutual fund category is different. You cannot say that a particular mutual fund category has a high risk or has a low risk based on a common scale or common parameter. Sure, if you invest in direct equity, then, in its comparison, equity mutual funds have low risk. But the risk associated with every mutual fund category is different. So, before investing in any Mutual Fund, check the viscometer of that particular mutual fund scheme. Every scheme has a risk assigned to it, and you can see what risks you will be taking.

2. Regular & Direct Plans

The second important point is that the Expense Ratio of Direct plans is less than regular plans. Because of this, Direct plans generate better returns in comparison to Regular plans.

Now, some investors are under the impression that direct plans and regular plans of Mutual Fund schemes are different. That's not true. These are just plans for the same scheme.

The only difference is that there is no agent or broker in between in the direct plans, so no commission or brokerage is applied. This means lower costs of the fund house and ultimately lower annual costs you need to pay for your investments. In the case of regular plans, you get complete services from Mutual fund distributors. Just like you need services for your washing m/c after you buy, in the case of mutual funds also need a different types of services, such as Portfolio review, rebalancing the portfolio, switches if required, unit transmission to the nominee in case of death, and so on. MF distributor serves you as and when you are needed.

3. You won't get the same returns every year

Normally when you hear Mutual Fund returns, they are annualized returns. This can give the impression that you will earn the same returns every year.

Suppose the annualized returns of a certain Mutual Fund Scheme are 12%. That doesn't mean you will earn 12% every year. That's because the returns of Mutual Funds are not linear. For example, a Mutual Fund Scheme may give you

+12% returns in the first year, while it may just give -2% in the second year. There might be periods of no returns too. So, you need to be prepared to see this variability in your annual returns. It is because of volatility in the market.

4. Consistency of returns is a hallmark of good funds

A particular Mutual Fund Scheme giving a 10% consistent return is better than a Mutual Fund Scheme which has given +17% returns in the first year and -10% returns in the second year. Now, why is this consistency in performance important? So that the losses can be controlled and you have a higher chance of earning good returns. For instance, a 5% fall in a year means the fund has to generate around 11% returns to cover the loss and give you a 5% return. For this reason, a consistent fund will generate better returns on an annualized basis on a long-term basis. So, always pick a consistent fund. A mutual fund advisor can support you in picking a good fund for a range of funds on the basis of his expertise.

5. SIPs Help Create Investing Discipline

Automated investing via SIPs not only helps teach discipline; they also help you benefit from market volatility. That's because when the market goes down, you get more units for the same price. This helps you bring down your overall cost of investing. This is called Rupee Cost Averaging, which can help you generate good returns in the long run.

6. Asset Allocation and Periodic Rebalancing are Crucial

Never keep you're all your eggs in one basket is a saying. And this is true when it comes to investing. Asset allocation is the process of dividing your investments across asset classes to reduce your portfolio risk. So before you start investing, decide how much you will invest in different asset classes likeequities, gold, debt, etc., and then invest. And while assetallocation is crucial, it won't be as beneficial as it can be with rebalancing. Rebalancing means that whenever an asset class runs up and its percentage in your portfolio goes up, you book profits from it and reinvest that money in other asset classes that are part of your portfolio. For asset allocation and rebalancing of portfolio always take the help of Mutual fund advisors as they know the better way to do it.

Know before investing.

Before investing in mutual funds you need to think of your risk-taking capacity, your financial goals or purpose of investing, time horizon to achieve your financial goal. Once you are clear of all the above you can choose a suitable fund to invest in it. Before making any investment it is mandatory to be KYC compliant, if you are not, you need to submit a PAN card, Address proof, photo with the KYC application form.

It is always better to have your own advisor or MFD who is well informed of all Do's and Don'ts of mutual fund and he/she take care of your all investments, documentation, reviews, and keeps all records.

Know your financial goals.

When we ask people about their financial goal or purpose of investment, most of them do not know. It is very simple that when money is spent to get the desired thing, spent on any ceremony, buying a property, spent on education or marriage of kids or for regular income after retirement is few financial goals or purpose one can decide before making an investment.

"Investing without a goal is just like you are playing football without a goal post."

"Investing without a goal is just like you are driving a car without a destination."

Know your financial goals.

DREAM BIG
SET GOALS
MAKE A PLAN
TAKE ACTION

A saving and investment plan can help you meet your goals, strategic use of credit and debt, coupled with adequate insurance to protect you and your family. If you have not planned for your finances properly it may hurt you when there is – loss of job, unexpected emergency expenses, rising health care costs or loss in your investment portfolio, etc. If you have done strong financial planning upon which you rely, you get peace of mind and so having financial planning provide you a sense of financial freedom too.

Setting your financial goals:

Before starting any investment, identify your goals which are very important and will be a pillar of your investment, estimate the future cost of that goal, time horizon to achieve the goal, and the type of investment that may be suitable for accumulating the money you will need for achievement of your financial goal.

Know your financial goals.

Financial goals depend upon the purpose of use of money that will be accumulated over a number of years. So it is very important to set a time horizon for every goal. The goals canbe divided into 3 types based on the horizon of the goal as under:

Short-term goals: If you need your money to be spent in thenext few years then it is to be invested carefully. Your focus must be on taking very little risk and protecting your capital. You need to be sure that your money is secure and accessibleor you can check its returns. For example, buying a car, making a down payment for a home loan, traveling for vacation, getting married, starting a business, etc. can be your short-term financial goals.

Mid-term goals: If you need your money back after about 5-7 years down the line, you shall be careful to invest where there will be reasonable growth and financial security. For example, payment for children's education, buying a second home, traveling to a foreign tour or to a special destination, etc.

Long-term goals: You must have a perfect financial plan for your major financial goals to be achieved in the next 10+ years down the financial journey. For example: Living stress-free in Retirement age, for expenses of travel and hobbies, for long-term health care, creating a legacy, Kid's higher education, and their marriage, etc.

Your financial goals must be SMART enough so that you can achieve them.

S – Specific: Specific in amount, dates, and resources.
M – Measurable: Measurable in an amount in Rupees Needed to achieve goals.
A – Attainable: Attainable in the time frame and income level.
R – Realistic: Your goals need to be doable based on your circumstances.
T – Time-Oriented: Create a timeline to achieve your goals.

You need to have time on a regular basis to monitor the progress of your financial goals at least once in 6 months or once in a year after investment as per financial goals. You can review the progress of your financial goals with the help of your financial advisor if it is architected by him.

What are Mutual Funds?

Mutual funds are collections of stocks, bonds and other financial assets that are managed by a professional investment company. In a mutual fund scheme pool of money is collected from many peoples and financial institutions and a fund manager decides the amount of money to be invested as per the objective of the scheme with an aim to increase the value of each stock of the fund for the investors. The gain on the investment is passed on to investors.

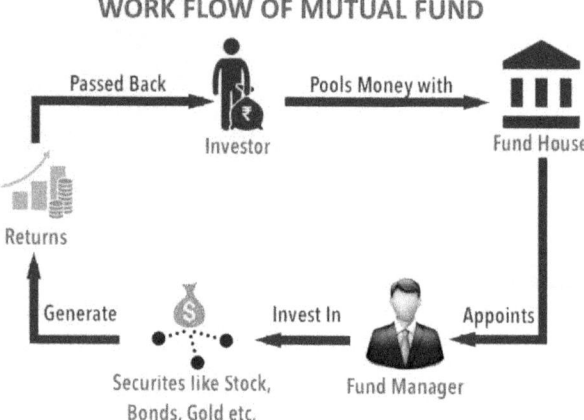

Various objects of Mutual Fund: There are many different types of mutual fund schemes; each has its own objective. For example, the object of the scheme could be capital appreciation over a long period of time, which can fulfill your long-term financial goals. There are a lot of schemes where an investor can invest in. However he should not rush to invest without knowing its category, the risk involved the orientation of the scheme, the types of asset classes the scheme will invest in and fund manager's style of investment, etc.

Asset Classes: Mutual fund schemes can be classified on the basis of their asset classes in which money will be invested on behalf of investors. Such as Equity, Debt, Equity and Debt, Gold, Government bonds, etc. There are funds invested in Equity and Debt, these are called Hybrid Equity funds. If it invests in a purely Equity fund then it is called is Equity oriented fund and its money is invested in more than two asset classes such as Equity, Debt, Gold, Real estate, these type of schemes are classified as Multicap Funds.

Types of Mutual Fund and its categories: Broadly MF schemes can be dived into two categories:

1. **Open-ended:** These schemes are always open for buying and selling of units.
2. **Close-ended:** These schemes are open for buying of units only during the new fund offer period and then after that period is over new investor cannot invest in it. The scheme is close to the stated period and gets mature after the completion of the period. There are funds that are actively managed and those are that passive. Passive funds track their popular index. Once you know which fund falls under which category, you can choose a scheme as per your risk and needs.

Equity Funds	Debt Funds	Hybrid Funds
Money invested purely In equity stocks. For eg.: Large cap, Mid cap, Small cap etc.	Money invested purely in debt Instruments. For eg.: Liquid fund, Ultra Short term fund, Credit risk funds etc.	Money invested in Equity stocks as well as in debt Instruments. For eg.: Hybrid funds, Balanced advantage etc.

You can understand all types of scheme categories above from a pyramid given below. As you go up in the period the risk increases in that scheme.

What are Mutual Funds?

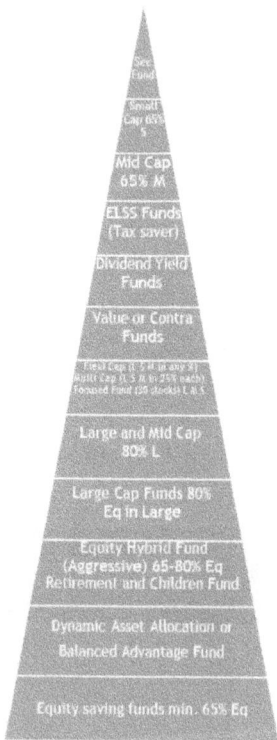
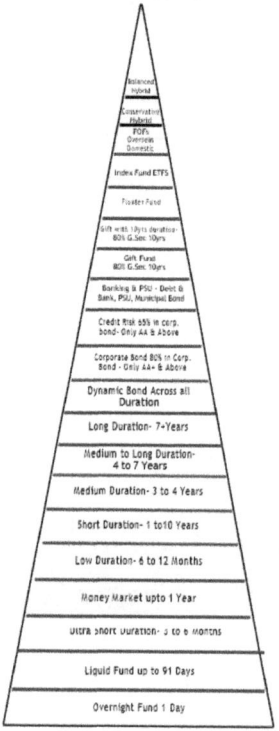

EQUITY FUNDS PYRAMID & **DEBT HYBRIDE PYRAMID**

SEBI categorization of Mutual Fund Schemes

As per SEBI guidelines on Categorization and Rationalization of schemes issued in October 2017, mutual fund schemes are classified as –

1. Equity Schemes
2. Debt Schemes
3. Hybrid Schemes
4. Solution-Oriented Schemes –For Retirement and Children

5. Other Schemes – Index Funds & ETFs and Fund of Funds

    – Under the Equity category, Large, Mid, and Small-capstocks have now been defined.

    –Naming convention of the schemes, especially debt schemes, as per the risk level of underlying portfolio (e.g., the erstwhile 'Credit Opportunity Fund' is now called "Credit Risk Fund")

    – Balanced / Hybrid funds are further categorized into conservative hybrid funds, balanced hybrid funds and aggressive hybrid funds.

Equity Schemes

An equity Scheme is a fund that –

- Primarily invests in equities and equity-related instruments.
- Seeks long-term growth but could be volatile in the short term.
- Suitable for investors with a higher risk appetite and longer investment horizon.

The objective of an equity fund is generally to seek long-term capital appreciation. Equity funds may focus on certain sectors of the market or may have a specific investment style, such as investing in value or growth stocks.

Equity Fund Categories as per SEBI guidelines on Categorization and Rationalization of schemes

Multi Cap Fund*	At least 65% investment in equity & equity related instruments
Large Cap Fund	At least 80% investment in large-cap stocks
Large & Mid Cap Fund	At least 35% investment in large-cap stocks and 35% in mid cap stocks
Mid Cap Fund	At least 65% investment in mid-cap stocks
Small cap Fund	At least 65% investment in small cap stocks
Dividend Yield Fund	Predominantly invest in dividend-yielding stocks, with at least 65% in stocks
Value Fund	Value investment strategy, with at least 65% in stocks
Contra Fund	Scheme follows contrarian investment strategy with at least 65% in stocks
Focused Fund	Focused on the number of stocks (maximum 30) with at least 65% in equity & equity related instruments
Sector / Thematic Fund	At least 80% investment in stocks of a particular sector/theme
ELSS	At least 80% in stocks in accordance with Equity Linked Saving Scheme, 2005, notified by Ministry of Finance

*Also referred to as Diversified Equity Funds – as they invest across stocks of different sectors and segments of the market. Diversification minimizes the risk of high exposure to a few stocks, sectors, or segments.

Sector-Specific Funds

Sector funds invest in a particular sector of the economy such as infrastructure, banking, technology or pharmaceuticals, etc.

- Since these funds focus on just one sector of the economy, they limit diversification and are thus riskier.
- Timing of investment into such funds is important because the performance of the sectors tends to be cyclical.

Examples of Sector Specific Funds - Equity Mutual Funds with an investment objective to invest in

- Pharma & Healthcare Sector. Banking & Finance Sector.
- FMCG (fast-moving consumer goods) and related sectors. Technology and related sectors.

Thematic Funds

- Thematic funds select stocks of companies in industries that belong to a particular theme - For example, Infrastructure, Service industries, PSUs, or MNCs.
- They are more diversified than Sector Funds and hence have lower risk than Sector funds.

Value Funds (Strategy and Style Based Funds)

- Equity funds may be categorized based on the valuation parameters adopted in-stock selection, such as
  - Growth funds identify momentum stocks that are expected to perform better than the market
  - Value funds identify stocks that are currently undervalued but are expected to perform well over time as the value is unlocked

- Equity funds may hold a concentrated portfolio to benefit from stock selection.
  - These funds will have a higher risk since the effect of a wrong selection can be substantial on the portfolio's return

Contra Funds

- Contra funds are equity mutual funds that take a contrarian view of the market.
- Underperforming stocks and sectors are picked at low price points with a view that they will perform in the long run.
- The portfolios of contra funds have defensive and beaten- down stocks that have given negative returns during bear markets.
- These funds carry the risk of getting calls wrong as catching a trend before the herd is not possible in every market cycle and these funds typically underperform in a bull market.
- As per the SEBI guidelines on Scheme categorization of mutual funds, a fund house can either offer a Contra Fund or a Value Fund, not both.

Equity Linked Savings Schemes (ELSS)

ELSS invests at least 80% in stocks in accordance with Equity Linked Saving Scheme, 2005, notified by the Ministry of Finance.

- Has lock-in period of 3 years (which is shortest amongst all other tax saving options)
- Currently eligible for deduction under Sec 80C of the Income Tax Act up to ₹1,50,000

DEBT SCHEMES

- A debt fund (also known as an income fund) is a fund that invests primarily in bonds or other debt securities.
- Debt funds invest in short and long-term securities issued by the government, public financial institutions, companies
    - Treasury bills, Government Securities, Debentures, Commercial paper, Certificates of Deposit and others
- Debt funds can be categorized based on the tenor of the securities held in the portfolio and/or on the basis of the issuers of the securities or their fund management strategies, such as
    - Short-term funds, Medium-term funds, Long-term funds, Gilt fund, Treasury fund, corporate bond fund, Infrastructure debt fund
- Floating rate funds, Dynamic Bond funds, Fixed MaturityPlans
- Debt funds have potential for income generation andcapital preservation.

Debt fund categories as per SEBI guidelines on Categorization and Rationalization of schemes

Overnight Fund	Overnight securities having maturity of 1 day
Liquid Fund	Debt and money market securities with maturity of up to 91 days only
Ultra Short Duration Fund	Debt & Money Market instruments with Macaulay duration of the portfolio between 3 months - 6 months

Low Duration Fund	Investment in Debt & Money Market instruments with Macaulay duration portfolio between 6 months- 12 months
Money Market Fund	Investment in Money Market instruments having maturity up to 1 Year
Short Duration Fund	Investment in Debt & Money Market instruments with Macaulay duration of the portfolio between 1 year - 3 years
Medium Duration Fund	Investment in Debt & Money Market instruments with Macaulay duration of portfolio between 3 years - 4 years
Medium to Long Duration Fund	Investment in Debt & Money Market instruments with Macaulay duration of the portfolio between 4 - 7 years
Long Duration Fund	Investment in Debt & Money Market Instruments with Macaulay duration of the portfolio greater than 7 years
Dynamic Bond	Investment across duration
Corporate Bond Fund	Minimum 80% investment in corporate bonds only in AA+ and above rated corporate bonds
Credit Risk Fund	Minimum 65% investment in corporate bonds, only in AA and below rated corporate bonds
Banking andPSU Fund	Minimum 80% in Debt instruments of banks, Public Sector Undertakings, Public Financial Institutions andMunicipal Bonds
Gilt Fund	Minimum 80% in G-secs, across maturity
Gilt Fund with 10 year constant Duration	Minimum 80% in G-secs, such that the Macaulayduration of the portfolio is equal to 10 years

Floater Fund	Minimum 65% in floating rate instruments (including fixed rate instruments converted to floating rate exposures using swaps/ derivatives)

Dynamic Bond funds alter the tenor of the securities in the portfolio in line with expectations on interest rates. The tenor is increased if interest rates are expected to go down and vice versa

Floating rate funds invest in bonds whose interests are reset periodically so that the fund earns coupon income that is in line with current rates in the market, and eliminates interest rate risk to a large extent

Short-Term Debt Funds

The primary focus of short-term debt funds is coupon income. Short-term debt funds have to also be evaluated for the credit risk they may take to earn higher coupon income. The tenor of the securities will define the return and risk of the fund.

- Funds holding securities with lower tenors have lower risk and lower returns.

- Liquid funds invest in securities with not more than 91 days to maturity.
- Ultra Short-Term Debt Funds hold a portfolio with a slightly higher tenor to earn higher coupon income.

Short-Term Fund combine coupon income earned from a predominantly short-term debt portfolio with some exposure to longer term securities to benefit from appreciation in price.

Fixed Maturity Plans (FMPs)

- FMPs are closed-ended funds which eliminate interest rate risk and lock-in a yield by investing only in securities whose maturity matches the maturity of the fund.

- FMPs create an investment portfolio whose maturity profile match that of the FMP tenor.
- Potential to provide better returns than liquid funds and Ultra Short Term Funds since investments are locked in
- Low mark to market risk as investments are liquidated at maturity.
- Investors commit money for a fixed period.
- Investors cannot prematurely redeem the units from the fund
- FMPs, being closed-end schemes are mandatorily listed - investors can buy or sell units of FMPs only on the stock exchange after the NFO.
- Only Units held in dematerialized mode can be traded; therefore investors seeking liquidity in such schemes need to have a demat account.

Capital Protection Oriented Funds

Capital Protection Oriented Funds are close-ended hybrid funds that create a portfolio of debt instruments and equity derivatives

- The portfolio is structured to provide capital protection and is rated by a credit rating agency on its ability to do so. The rating is reviewed every quarter.
- The debt component of the portfolio has to be invested in instruments with the highest investment grade rating.

- A portion of the amount brought in by the investors is invested in debt instruments that are expected to mature to the par value of the capital invested by investors into the fund. The capital is thus protected.
- The remaining portion of the funds is used to invest in equity derivatives to generate higher returns.

HYBRID FUNDS

Hybrid funds Invest in a mix of equities and debt securities.

SEBI has classified Hybrid funds into 7 sub- categories as follows:

Conservative Hybrid Fund	10% to 25% investment in equity & equity related instruments; and 75% to 90% in Debt instruments
Balanced Hybrid Fund	40% to 60% investment in equity & equity related instruments; and 40% to 60% in Debt instruments
Aggressive Hybrid Fund	65% to 80% investment in equity & equity related instruments; and 20% to 35% in Debt instruments
Dynamic Asset Allocation or Balanced Advantage Fund	Investment in equity/ debt that is managed dynamically (0% to 100% in equity & equity related instruments; and 0% to 100% in Debt instruments)
Multi Asset Allocation Fund	Investment in at least 3 asset classes with a minimum allocation of at least 10% in each asset class

Arbitrage Fund	Scheme following arbitrage strategy, with minimum 65% investment in equity & equity related instruments
Equity Savings	Equity and equity-related instruments (min.65%); debt instruments (min.10%) and derivatives (min. for hedging to be specified in the SID)

Solution-oriented & other funds

Retirement Fund	Lock-in for at least 5 years or till retirement age whichever is earlier
Children's Fund	Lock-in for at least 5 years or till the child attains age of majority whichever is earlier
Index Funds/ ETFs	Minimum 95% investment in securities of a particular index
Fund of Funds (Overseas/ Domestic)	Minimum 95% investment in the underlying fund(s)

Hybrid funds

Invest in a mix of equities and debt securities. They seek to find a 'balance' between growth and income by investing in both equity and debt.

- The regular income earned from the debt instruments provides greater stability to the returns from such funds.
- The proportion of equity and debt that will be held in the portfolio is indicated in the Scheme Information Document

- Equity-oriented hybrid funds (Aggressive Hybrid Funds) are ideal for investors looking for growth in their investment with some stability.
- Debt-oriented hybrid funds (Conservative Hybrid Fund) are suitable for conservative investors looking for a boost in returns with a small exposure to equity.
- The risk and return of the fund will depend upon the equity exposure taken by the portfolio - Higher the allocation to equity, the greater is the risk

Multi Asset Funds

- A multi-asset fund offers exposure to a broad number of asset classes, often offering a level of diversification typically associated with institutional investing.
- Multi-asset funds may invest in a number of traditional equity and fixed income strategies, index-tracking funds, financial derivatives as well as commodities like gold.
- This diversity allows portfolio managers to potentially balance risk with reward and deliver steady, long-term returns for investors, particularly in volatile markets.

Arbitrage Funds

"Arbitrage" is the simultaneous purchase and sale of an asset to take advantage of the price differential in the two markets and profit from the price difference of the asset on different markets or in different forms.

- Arbitrage fund buys a stock in the cash market and simultaneously sells it in the Futures market at a higher price to generate returns from the difference in the price of the security in the two markets.

- The fund takes equal but opposite positions in both the markets, thereby locking in the difference.
- The positions have to be held until the expiry of the derivative cycle and both positions need to be closed at the same price to realize the difference.
- The cash market price converges with the Futures market price at the end of the contract period. Thus it delivers risk- free profit for the investor/trader.
- Price movements do not affect the initial price differential because the profit in one market is set off by the loss in the other market.
- Since mutual funds invest their own funds, the difference is fully the return.

Hence, Arbitrage funds are considered to be a good choice for cautious investors who want to benefit from a volatile market without taking on too much risk.

Index Funds

Index funds create a portfolio that mirrors a market index.

- The securities included in the portfolio and their weights are the same as those in the index
- The fund manager does not rebalance the portfolio based on their view of the market or sector
- Index funds are passively managed, which means that the fund manager makes only minor, periodic adjustments to keep the fund in line with its index. Hence, an Index fund offers the same return and risk represented by the index it tracks.
- The fees that an index fund can charge is capped at 1.5% Investors have the comfort of knowing the

stocks that will form part of the portfolio since the composition of the index isknown.

Exchange Traded Funds (ETFs)

An ETF is a marketable security that tracks an index, a commodity, bonds, or a basket of assets like an index fund.

- ETFs are listed on stock exchanges.
- Unlike regular mutual funds, an ETF trades like a common stock on a stock exchange. The traded price of an ETF changes throughout the day like any other stock, as it is bought and sold on the stock exchange.
- ETF Units are compulsorily held in Demat mode
- ETFs are passively managed, which means that the fund manager makes only minor, periodic adjustments to keep the fund in line with its index
- Because an ETF tracks an index without trying to outperform it, it incurs lower administrative costs than actively managed portfolios.
- Rather than investing in an 'active' fund managed by a fund manager, when one buys units of an ETF one is harnessing the power of the market itself.
- Suitable for investors seeking returns similar to index and liquidity similar to stocks

Fund of Funds (FoF)

- Fund of funds is mutual fund schemes that invest in the units of other schemes of the same mutual fund or othermutual funds.
- The schemes selected for investment will be based on the investment objective of the FoF

- The FoF has two levels of expenses: that of the scheme whose units the FoF invests in and the expense of the FoF itself. Regulations limit the total expenses that can be charged across both levels as follows:
  - TER in respect of FoF investing liquid schemes, indexfunds & ETFs has been capped @ 1%
  - TER of FoF investing in equity-oriented schemes has been capped @ 2.25%
  - TER of FoF investing in other schemes than mentioned above has been capped at @2%.

Gold Exchange Traded Funds (FoF)

- Gold ETFs are ETFs with gold as the underlying asset
  - The scheme will issue units against gold held. Each unit will represent a defined weight in gold, typically one gram.
  - The scheme will hold gold in form of physical gold orgold-related instruments approved by SEBI.
  - Schemes can invest up to 20% of net assets in the GoldDeposit Scheme of banks
- The price of ETF units moves in line with the price of gold on metal exchange.
- After the NFO, units are issued to intermediaries called authorized participants against gold or funds submitted. They can also redeem the units for the underlying gold.

Benefits of Gold ETFs

- Convenience --> option of holding gold electronicallyinstead of physical gold.

- Safer option to hold gold since there are no risks of theft or purity.
- Provides easy liquidity and ease of transaction.
- Gold ETFs are treated as non-equity-oriented mutual funds for the purpose of taxation.
  - Eligible for long-term capital gains benefits if held for three years.
  - No wealth tax is applicable on Gold ETFs

International Funds

- International funds enable investments in markets outside India, by holding in their portfolio one or more of the following:
  - Equity of companies listed abroad.
  - ADRs and GDRs of Indian companies.
  - Debt of companies listed abroad.
  - ETFs of other countries.
  - Units of passive index funds in other countries.
  - Units of actively managed mutual funds in other countries.
- International equity funds may also hold some of their portfolios in Indian equity or debt.
  - They can hold some portion of the portfolio in money market instruments to manage liquidity.
- International funds give the investor additional benefits of
  - Diversification, since global markets may have a low correlation with domestic markets.

- Investment options that may not be available domestically.
- Access to companies that are global leaders in their field.
* There are risks associated with investing in such funds, such as:
  - Political events and macro-economic factors are less familiar and therefore difficult to interpret.
  - Movements in the foreign exchange rate may affect the return on redemption.
  - Countries may change their investment policy towards global investors.
* For the purpose of taxation, these funds are considered as non-equity-oriented mutual fund schemes.

Mutual fund Investment options: There are three options to be selected after selecting a scheme of the mutual funds.

1. **Growth:** In this option, the scheme does not pay unless you redeem but the scheme's NAV continue to grow till you are invested. The NAV rises as the market rises due to profit made by the Fund manager by selling the underlying stocks at high and buying at low. The number of units remains the same for one-time investment and in the case of SIP, units are added every month.

2. **DCW Payout** (Income distribution cum capital withdrawal): It was earlier known as the Dividend option but regulation has changed it to a better understanding of investors. In this option, scheme money is paid from the profit made by the scheme as and when there is a surplus of profit. IDCW can pay

monthly, quarterly, half-yearly, or yearly. You should be aware that IDCW is not guaranteed, which means it is not bond to payout.

3. **IDCW Reinvest:** It is very similar to IDCW payout but the only difference is that in this option money of IDCW is reinvested in the same scheme by purchasing more units on your behalf at the present NAV and in this way number of units rises.

It is very important to choose options wisely. As investors, the treatment of gain and taxes are two important factors that make difference in the above options. If we evaluate returns from investment there is no difference in the above3 options. The difference will be in respect to the applicable taces.

So it is important to consider the tax impact while selecting from the above options, because of long term and short term holding period. The tax treatment also differs for Equity and Debt schemes.

Advantages and disadvantages of Mutual Fund.

People who have invested in mutual funds for a long period of time know that they are the best investment options to achieve financial goals. Despite the rising popularity of mutual funds in India, there are many investors, who are not aware of the benefits and disadvantages of mutual funds. There are also several misconceptions regarding mutual funds in our country. For example, a lot of people associate mutual funds with the share market only. Mutual fund investment is not limited to investing in the share market only; through mutual funds, you can also invest in the debt market, money market, gold, etc. We believe that, if people's awareness of mutual funds increases,

Advantages and disadvantages of Mutual Fund.

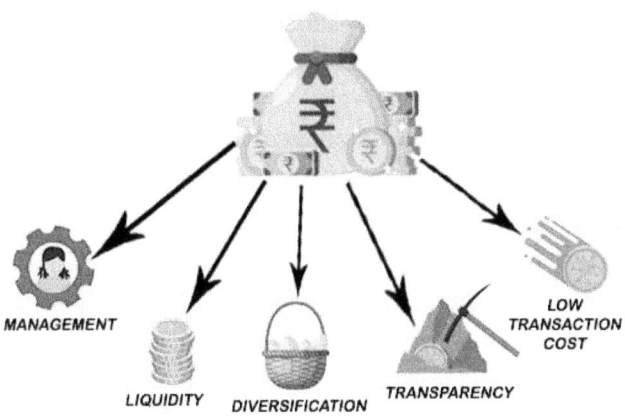

People who have invested in mutual funds for a long period of time know that they are the best investment options to achieve financial goals. Despite the rising popularity of mutual funds in India, there are many investors, who are not aware of the benefits and disadvantages of mutual funds. There are also several misconceptions regarding mutual funds in our country. For example, a lot of people associate mutual funds with the share market only. Mutual fund investment is not limited to investing in the share market only; through mutual funds, you can also invest in the debt market, money market, gold, etc. We believe that, if people's awareness of mutual funds increases, then more and more people will use mutual funds as the most important asset in their financial planning. Let us see the major benefits of investing in mutual funds.

1. **Professional Management-** Investors may not have the time or the required knowledge and resources to conduct their research and purchase individual stocks or bonds. A mutual fund is managed by full-time, professional money managers who have the expertise, experience and resources to actively buy,

sell, and monitor investments. A fund manager continuously monitors investments and rebalances the portfolio accordingly to meet the scheme's objectives. Portfolio management by professional fund managers is one of the most important advantages of a mutual fund.

2. **Risk Diversification-** Buying shares in a mutual fund is an easy way to diversify your investments across many securities and asset categories such as equity, debt, and gold, which helps in spreading the risk - so you won't have all your eggs in one basket. This proves to be beneficial when the underlying security of a given mutual fund scheme experiences market headwinds. With diversification, the risk associated with one asset class is countered by the others. Even if one investment in the portfolio decreases in value, other investments may not be impacted and may even increase in value. In other words, you don't lose out on the entire value of your investment if a particular component of your portfolio goes through a turbulent period. Thus, risk diversification is one of the most prominent advantages of investing in mutual funds.

3. **Affordability & Convenience (Invest Small Amounts)-** For many investors, it could be more costly to directly purchase all of the individual securities held by a single mutual fund. By contrast, the minimum initial investments for most mutual funds are more affordable.

4. **Liquidity-** You can easily redeem (liquidate) units of open-ended mutual fund schemes to meet your financial needs on any business day (when the stock markets and/or banks are open), so you have easy access to your

money. Upon redemption, the redemption amount is credited in your bank account within one day to 3-4 days, depending upon the type of scheme e.g., in respect of Liquid Funds and Overnight Funds, the redemption amount is paid out the next business day.

However, please note that units of close-ended mutual fund schemes can be redeemed only on maturity. Likewise, units of ELSS have a 3-year lock-in period and can be liquidated only thereafter.

5. **Low Cost-** An important advantage of mutual funds is their low cost. Due to huge economies of scale, mutual funds schemes have a low expense ratio. The expense ratio represents the annual fund operating expenses of a scheme, expressed as a percentage of the fund's daily net assets. Operating expenses of a scheme are administration, management, advertising-related expenses, etc. The limit of expense ratio for various types of schemes has been specified under Regulation 52 of SEBI Mutual Fund Regulations, 1996.

6. **Well-Regulated-** Mutual Funds are regulated by the capital markets regulator, Securities, and Exchange Board of India (SEBI) under SEBI (Mutual Funds) Regulations, 1996. SEBI has laid down stringent rules and regulations keeping investor protection, transparency with appropriate risk mitigation framework and fair valuation principles.

7. **Tax Benefits-** Investment in ELSS up to ₹1,50,000 qualifies for tax benefit under section 80C of the Income Tax Act, 1961. Mutual Fund investments when held for a longer term are tax-efficient. Investment done in Equity linked saving scheme (ELSS) has a lock-in

period of 3 years. Only after the completion of 3 years, one can redeem from the ELSS scheme.

8. **Suitability for a variety of financial goals-** Mutual funds are suitable for a wide variety of financial goals and risk profiles. Equity funds are ideal for long-term financial goals. Balanced funds are great long-term investment options for investors having moderate risk profiles. Long-term debt funds are good investment options for medium-term financial goals, while short-term debt funds are good investment options for short-term financial goals.

Mutual funds provide great solutions for even very short term (few days, weeks, or months) financial goals. Liquid funds are a much better vehicle for parking your short-term funds for a few days to a few weeks or even months, compared to your savings bank account. Liquid fund returns, which are based on money market rates, are much higher than your savings bank interest rate. Ultra-short term debt funds offer investment solutions for periods ranging from a few months up to a year.

The returns of ultra-short-term debt funds are usually higher than liquid funds. One can also consider arbitrage funds for parking short-term funds. Arbitrage funds, on a historical basis, have matched liquid fund returns, but are more tax-efficient than liquid and ultra-short-term debt funds.

There are mutual fund schemes for every kind of return and risk level and for every kind of time horizon. No matter which kind of investment you want there is a variety of schemes that will suit your need.

Disadvantages of Mutual Funds

1. **Costs:** You must be surprised to see 'cost' both as an advantage and disadvantage of mutual funds! Some mutual funds have high costs associated with them and if you exit before the stipulated period, then you also incur exit load charges.

   The salary of the market analysts and fund managers comes from the investors along with the operational costs of the fund. Total fund management charges are one of the first parameters to consider when choosing a mutual fund. Higher management fees do not guarantee better fund performance.

2. **Dilution of Funds:** The biggest disadvantage of a mutual fund is diversification. Diversification has an averaging effect on your investments. It saves you from suffering major losses, But as a result of this, it also prevents you from making any major gains! Hence, It is recommended that you do not invest in too many mutual funds and over-diversify the portfolio. While diversification averages your risks of loss, it can also dilute your profits. Hence, you should not invest in many mutual funds at a time. The benefits of mutual funds can undoubtedly override the disadvantages if you make informed choices.

3. **Lock-in Period:** Another disadvantage of Mutual funds is that some mutual funds are like ELSS funds and come with a lock-in period of three years. During this lock-in period, you cannot withdraw your invested amount for 3 years. Additionally, if you invest in close-ended funds, then you will not be able to liquidate these investments in case of any emergencies.

4. **Fluctuating Returns (Volatility):** Mutual fund returns are not guaranteed and keep on fluctuating as per the market. Hence investors need to be aware of the risk profile of the fund before investing.
5. **Exit Loads:** You have exit load as fees charged by AMCs when exiting a mutual fund. It discourages investors from redeeming investments for some time. It also helps the fund manager garner the required funds to purchase the appropriatesecurities at the right price and time.

Key Takeaways on the Disadvantages of Mutual Funds:

- Exit loads are applicable if you sell your investments within a specified time period.
- Mutual funds are subject to market risk and are notguaranteed.
- Some mutual funds come with a lock-in period of 3years.

Final Thoughts

However, investors may not have the time, knowledge, or patience to research and analyses different mutual funds.

You must take a detailed look at the crucial advantages of mutual funds and the disadvantages of investing in mutual funds before making an investment decision. Once you decide to invest in mutual funds, the real difficulty lies in deciding which mutual fund to invest in as per your financial goal. You can take the help of your financial or mutual fund advisor to choose a suitable mutual fund schemes for your financial goal.

Principles of Mutual Fund Investing

For new investors, it is better to know the following concepts of Mutual Funds before they start their investment.

1. **Risk:** Before investing in mutual funds every investor should know their risk-taking capacity. For instance, at what level of risk are you comfortable? Are you a conservative investor? Who does not want to risk losing any of his capital? Moderate investors, who want to protect their assets while increasing the value of the portfolio. Aggressive investors, who are ready to take risks with achieving more than average returns on their portfolio.

   As your financial goals and priorities change, you may need to modify your investing style or risk. For example, if your retirement is in near future, you may want to shift from an aggressive to the moderate or conservative style of investing.

Every investor new or experienced must know risk andreward, the Time Value of Money, diversification, real returns, and other concepts that are base of good investment planning.

2. **Risk-Return relationship:** "Higher the risk, higher will be reward and vice versa: Using this principle, low levels of uncertainty (risk) are associated with potential returns and a higher level of risk with high potential returns.

    If you take a higher risk, your investment needs to be invested for a higher duration and if you take the lower risk, your risk your investment can be for a lower duration. So you must know your risk and investment horizon to get desired returns.

Time Vs Returns	
Period	**Return %**
1-2 Years	5
2-5 Years	8
5-10 Years	12
10-20 Years	15
20-30 Years	18

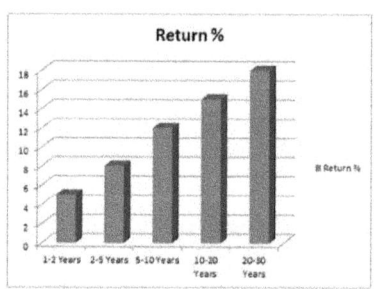

Risk Vs Reward Vs Time (Only for understanding)

3. **Diversification:** Diversification is a tool to reduce risk by allocating your investments across various financial assets, classes, industries, and other categories. **("Don't put all the eggs in the one basket").** Its goal is to maximize returns by investing in different areas which

react differently to the same event. For example, if you wish to invest Rs. 1 Lakh inequity and by any reason market tumbles down to 50%, your investment value will behalf. Now if you split your investment of 1 lakh between Equity and Debt, drop of 50% equity market and debt remain same your investment value will be 75,000/- and not 50,000/-. So by diversification into debt, youmanaged to provide protection to your capital.

4. **Return on investment:** It is the amount you get back on your investment. Your return on your investment should be positive with capital intact. Investing in stocks, bonds or mutual fund schemes carries more or less amount of risk because that your return can be negative. For example, you bought mutual fund units for Rs. 30/- NAV and sell it for Rs.35/-, you get Rs.5/- per unit minus expense ratio of that scheme or taxes as per law. But you may incur a loss of Rs.5 /- on your investment if you sell it at Rs.30 /- NAV (not counting expenses & taxes). So the total returns are equal to gain or loss in value plus investment earning.

5. **Rate of Return (RoR):** It is the net gain or loss on an investment over a specific time period, expressed as % of investment cost.

$$RoR = \frac{\text{Current Value} - \text{Original Value}}{\text{Original Value}} \times 100$$

For example, Compare a return of Rs.5/- per unit on Rs.30/- investment with a return of Rs.5/- per unit on Rs.60/- investment. In both cases, the return is the same, but your rate of return is not the same. Let's calculate for above both : ROR=35-30/30X100=16.67% and ROR=65-60/60X100=8.33%

6. **CAGR (Compounded Annualized Growth Rate):** It is the mean annual growth rate on your investment over a specified period of time longer than one year. It is one of the most correct methods to calculate returns for individual assets, portfolios and for anything that can be positive or negative in value over a time period.

$$CAGR = \left(\frac{\text{End Value - Start Value}}{\text{Start Value}}\right)^{1/t} - 1$$

For example: Start value on 3/1/2010 is Rs.2000/- and End value on 3/7/2017 is Rs. 5000/- So, CAGR = (3000-2000/2000)1/2738 days – 1 = 13.939%

7. **Risk-adjusted return:** It is a measurement to find how much return an investment will give with the level of risk associated with it. The investor can compare between high risk & low-risk returns on his investment. By calculating risk-adjusted return, you can judge whether you are expecting the highest gain with minimum risk involved &

8. **Real Return:** It is what you earned on an investment after accounting taxes and inflation. Real returns are lower than nominal returns, which do not subtract taxes and inflation. When calculating the real rate of return, follow these steps: Take the difference between nominal rate & the inflation rate as a whole number, then divide by 1 plus the inflation rate as expressed as a decimal. For example, the nominal rate of return is 7% (Rs.1750/25000) but your real rate of return is -0.926% (-250/27000).

In real-life, inflation erodes your returns. So an investment of Rs.10,000/- earning 5% pa adds Rs.500/- at the end of one year. But if inflation is 4%, it eats Rs.400/- out of Rs.500/- & you get only Rs.100/- in your hand. So it is very important to look for investments whose value will move up with inflation or it should be more than inflation.

$$\text{Real Rate of Return} = \left(\frac{1+\text{Nominal rate}}{1+\text{Inflation rate}}\right) - 1 = \left(\frac{1+0.06}{1+0.03}\right) - 1 = 2.91\%$$

9. **Liquidity:** When an asset or stock can be converted into ready cash without affecting its market price is called liquidity. Cash is the most liquid asset, while tangible items such as cars, houses, etc are less liquid. Current, quick, and cash ratios are used to measure liquidity.

For example, saving bank a/c, money market liquid fund, fixed deposit in a bank is highly liquid, which can be converted easily into cash. Real estate is ill liquid, which means could be hard to sell for the price you want at the time you need money. Pvt. Equity & hedge funds are also ill liquid during the lock-in period. So, at the time of investing your hard-earned money, you must know its liquidity.

10. **Compounding:** It is the process whereby interest is credited to an existing principal amount as well as to interest already paid. "Interest on interest is called compounding". The effect of compounding is to magnify returns to interest over a time, which is miracle of compounding.

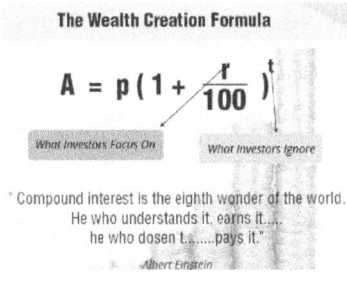

A= Final amount. P= Principal. r= Rate of interest. t= number of time periods elapsed.

Example: Monthly investment of Rs.5000/-, invested for 25 years, at a compounding rate of 12% pa, will grow to 94.88 lakh against a total investment of 15 lakh.

11. **Asset allocation:** It is an investment plan in which your aim is to balance your risk & reward by investing your total amount of money in equity, debt, and other asset classes such as gold, property, etc. Your investment plan must be designed to meet your financial goals, risk tolerance & horizon of financial goals. It is just like a balanced diet, you shall have a balanced investment portfolio to get an average return over a time period.

If you invest all your money in equity then surely it is highly risky & if you allocate your money into equity & debt you can reduce your risk. Asset allocation can be done in different asset classes, such as stocks, bonds, debt funds, equity funds, gold, real estate, Govt. securities, etc. You can build your portfolio with the help of **asset allocation** as an Aggressive, Moderate, or Conservative portfolio on the basis of your risk tolerance. By spreading your investments across different assets, you avoid being impacted by the poor performance of one asset class. This concept is known as Diversification. If you invest through mutual funds your diversification can be done very easily because in mutual funds you can invest in all kinds of assets through mutual fund schemes.

In this way, asset allocation helps you benefit from the different earning returns of different asset classes.

Example of asset allocation:

Investor's profile	Ideal asset allocation Debt %	Ideal asset allocation Equity %
Low risk	80-100	00-20
Conservative	60-80	20-40
Moderate	40-60	40-60
Aggressive	20-40	60-80
Very Aggressive	00-20	80-100

Understanding Risk Factors and market volatility

All the investments carry an element of hidden risk. Risk can be more or less, but without taking risk there is no reward. Knowing about the risk, it will make your investment decision incorrect way.

In mutual funds, you will get a risk meter to know the risk involved in any scheme.

1. **Low:** Principal at low risk.
2. **Low to moderate:** Principal at moderate-low risk.
3. **Moderate:** Principal at moderate risk.
4. **Moderately high:** Principal at moderately high risk.
5. **High:** Principal at high risk.

6. **Very high:** Principal at very high risk.

Risk is the uncertainty of return and a risk-return metrics helps to find uncertainty by providing an estimate of the range of possible returns.

Investore understand that their principal will be at moderate risk.

Risk is the uncertainty of return and risk-return metrics help to find uncertainty by providing an estimate of the range of possible returns.

Risk Tolerance: How much risk you can afford to take? The risk and return are fundamental to investments. The level of risk taken is also known as your risk profile. It depends on your personal and financial circumstances, your investment goals, and your emotions towards money. You can find your risk profile by answering the following questions:

How much RISK can you tolerate or take?

Q1. How old are you?

A: Under 35   **B:** 35-44

C: 45-54   **D:** 55 or above

Q2. What is the nature of your income?

A: Self-employed with a steady income.

B: Salaried employee with an established firm.

C: Self-employed with irregular income.

D: Salaried employee with a start-up.

Q3. How much of your current income goes towards loans?

A: 30-50%   **B:** More then 50%

C: 10-30%   **D:** 0-10%

Q4. How soon do you think you will start investments?

A: Not for another 10 Years.

B: Within the next 3 years.

C: In 3-7 years.

D: In 8-10 years.

Q5. What will you do if, during a market correction, one of your investments lost 30% of its value within weeks?

A: Sell the investment so you will not have to worry about afuture decline.

B: Buy more of the same, because it looks even better at correctprices than when you bought it.

C: Hold on to it and wait for it to bounce back.

Q6. If the market downturn continues, how long will you hold on to your portfolio before cashing in?

A: Another 6 months. **B:** At least a year.

C: A month **D:** Another 3 months.

Q7. Assuming you have some more money to invest now, how would you be willing to invest?

A: Wait for the market to recover 20% before investing a single rupee.

B: Invest in the market? No, thanks... I am out!

C: Invest some money in a staggered manner even if the market goes further down.

D: I don't mind putting in a large amount of money right away!

Q8. Given below are the likely Best and Worst annual returns of your investment. Which returns are most acceptable to you?

Avg Annual Returns		Best Annual Returns	Worst Annual Return
A	7.5%	12%	-5%
B	9%	18%	-12%
C	12%	25%	-20%
D	15%	40%	-35%

Scoring Matrix Answer Option

Question	A	B No	C	D	Your Score
1	4	3	2	1	
2	3	4	1	2	
3	2	1	3	4	
4	4	1	2	3	
5	1	3	2	-	
6	3	4	1	2	
7	2	1	3	4	
8	1	2	3	4	
Total Score					

Your Risk profile & Optimum Asset Allocation:

Risk Score and Investor risk profile	Equities	Ideal Asset Allocation Fixed Income/Debt	Gold
Below 20 Conservative	10-25%	60-70%	15-20%
20-25 Moderate	40-60%	30-45%	10-15%
Above 25 Aggressive	60-75%	20-30%	5-10%

Note: Make sure you stick to this risk profile even when the market goes on an extended rally. The only time you need to reassess the risk profile is if your personal circumstances change owing to any life event (marriage, birth of child, separation) or changes to income profile (large inheritance, job loss) or if financial goals are on the horizon.

Risk profiling is done by your financial advisor or experienced planner who looks at investors to arrive at their risk-taking capacity and sustainability.

Risk and Life stages: Your risk-taking capacity will vary as per your life stages & whether you want to grow your investment over a long period of time or need a regular income to maintain your lifestyle. You may take more riskin your younger life but as you grow old near to retirement you may like to take less risk & that your investment shallbe in defensive assets, such as hybrid or dynamic asset allocation funds or debt funds. This works well when the rate of interest is high & more than the rate of inflation. Butwhen it is the opposite, investors are exposed to inflation and long-term risk.

Inflation risk: It is a risk that the value of your investment will be eroded over a long period of time due to the rise in prices of commodities and thereby the rise in the cost of living. The real return on your investment is the amount you get after subtracting the inflation rate. (Real return= Rate of return on investment – rate of inflation) If you are earning an interest rate lower than the inflation rate, your real rate of return & purchasing power would decline over a long time. Inflation reduces your purchasing power; hence, today's money will not buy you the same thing tomorrow. Eg. 1 liter of milk which used to cost Rs.6/- in 1990, costs Rs.58/- today (2021) Investing in equities can help you beat inflation better than other asset classes & provides positive real returns over the long term. The real value of Rs.100/- will become Rs.11.34 in 30 years at an inflation of 7% p.a.

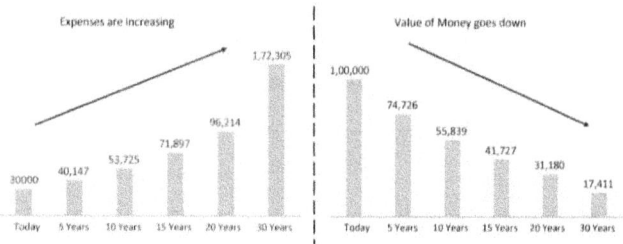

Be aware of inflation as inflation erodes wealth and purchasing power silently

Longevity risk: It is the risk that your savings will not be enough to cover your expenses during retirement. Average life expectancy is increasing and retirement corpus needs to be sufficient to provide you a regular income for 30 years or more. If you have invested large money in defensive assets, the risk of a shortfall in your retirement corpus couldincrease as the rate of interest falls.

Risk- Reward ratio: It is difficult to know the ratio between investment performance and risk. Higher returns are associated with a higher risk of price fluctuations. Risky investment is always volatile. It can very years to years. So,if you are staying invested in good funds, well-diversified assets, then the longer time of investment, the less will be volatile your returns, but there is no guarantee of what happened in the past will always happen in the future.

As per the history of the long run, equity is the asset class that has less volatility with the possibility of higher returns, although equity may incur big losses in short periods.

Correction is temporary, growth is permanent: One should not fear the volatility of the market, instead of maintaining the investment by staying focused on long-term economic & market expectations. Volatility is the nature of the market. Market movements are due to many reasons, such as changes in the global economy, natural disasters, world news flow, changes in Govt. policies, etc. Correction is not a fall in the market, rather it is a series of rising and fall in no particular order. Investors shall not fear any fall of the market but by staying invested they can earn more. Good investors look at every market fall as an opportunity to invest more due to the lower cost of investment. Investors shall have a longer investment time horizon and maintain a disciplined portfolio at the time of any correction of the market. At the time of any market fall investors shall not take any decision by emotions, it may cause then financial losses.

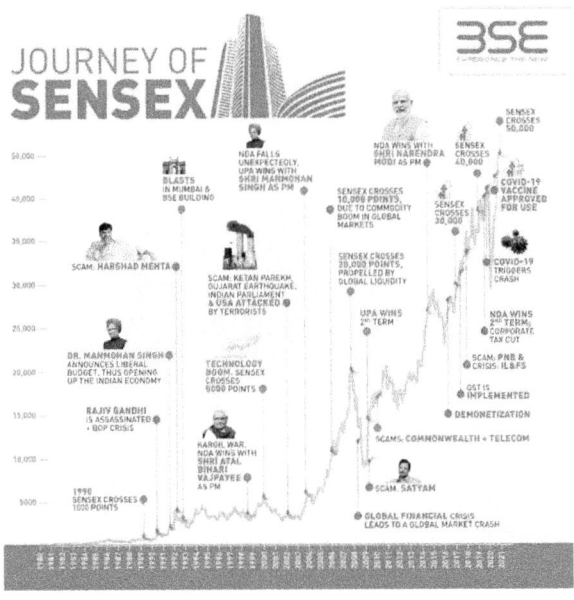

How to deal with volatility? : Looking at the present situation with clarity is the key to successful investment and not predicting the future. Volatility is more on daily basis but reduces on yearly basis. If you are increasing your investment holding period over years and decades, your return improves with your risk-return profile.

After every downfall, the market generally does rebound. Your investment return may affect due to your decision during market fall. So, investors who see volatility as a friend earn from those who see it as the enemy. A downfall in the market is an opportunity to build your portfolio by buying more units at lower costs. The market works like a roller coaster. When the market rises up you enjoy but when it comes down you fear it. A good investor always enjoys all downfalls and invests more to earn more and create wealth.

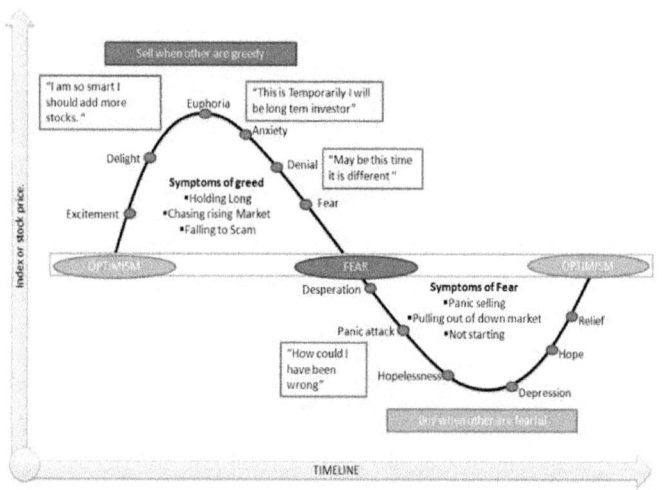

Important terms used in Mutual Fund.

Before investing it is very important for new investors to know the terms and their meaning used in the mutual fund industry. It will help investors to have a better knowledge of mutual fund concepts. By knowing the following important terms frequently used in mutual funds, investors will be able to make an informed decision of investing their hard-earned money.

Addendums and notices. (SID): Scheme Information Document is one of the many fund offer documents and has almost all the information about a mutual fund scheme; details like what are minimum subscription amounts, exit and entry loads, SIP details, fund managers and their experience, risk level, the objective of the scheme, etc.

Important terms used in Mutual Fund.

AMFI: The Association of Mutual Funds in India is an industry standards organization in India in the mutual fund sector. It was formed in 1995. Most mutual funds firms in India are its members. The organization aims to develop the mutual funds market in India, by improving ethical and professional standards.

AMC: An Asset Management Company (AMC) is a firm that invests the funds pooled from individual investors in securities with the objective of optimal return for investors in exchange for a fee. ... For example, a debt fund invests in bonds and risk-free Government bonds to maintain the minimum risk.

Folio number: In mutual funds, a folio number is a unique number identifying your account with the fund. A folio number also records items such as how much money each investor has placed with the fund, their transaction history, and contact details. A folio number can also be used to identify journal entries or parcels of land.

Transfer agent: Transfer agents work closely with registrars to ensure investors receive their due interest and dividend payments in a timely manner. Transfer agents' investment statements to mutual fund shareholders.

Trustee: A trustee in the case of Mutual funds is a holdingservice that has administrative power for managing the money, property, or assets used in mutual funds. The trustee can be an individual person, member of the board of directors, a company, or a bank appointed with the approval of the SECP. **Benchmark index:** A benchmark is a standard against which the performance of a security, mutual fund, or investment manager can be measured. Generally, broad market and market-segment stock and bond indexes are used for this purpose.

Important terms used in Mutual Fund.

CAGR: Compounded annual growth rate (CAGR) is one of the most commonly used terms in the mutual fund industry. CAGR represents the compounded growth rate of your investments made in mutual funds. It helps you gauge a mutual fund scheme's average annual growth over a giventime period.

Cash equivalent: Cash equivalents are investments securities that are meant for short-term investing; they have high credit quality and are highly liquid. Cash equivalents, also known as "cash and equivalents," are one of the three main asset classes in financial investing, along with stocks and bonds.

Credit risk: It is the risk of default of the issuer of the security in repaying the principal and/or interest Credit risk is higher with low-quality securities and therefore most conservative investors prefer mutual funds which invest only in high-credit quality debt securities.

Risk-adjusted returns: Risk-adjusted returns can likewise overseethe mailing of monthly help you measure the same. It is a concept that is used to measure an investment's return by examining how much risk is taken in obtaining the return. Risk-adjusted returns are useful for comparing various individual securities and mutual funds, as well as a portfolio.

Growth option: Some shares pay regular dividends, but by selecting a growth option, the mutual fund holder is allowing the fund company to reinvest the money it would otherwise payout to the investor in the form of a dividend. This money increases the net asset value (NAV) of the mutual fund.

Dividend option: In the dividend option of a mutual fund scheme, the profits made by the fund are distributed to the unit holders from time to time. The dividend option should be chosen if there is an expectation of periodic income from your investment without actually redeeming any of the units.

Dividend reinvests option: In the 'IDCW Reinvestment Option,' dividends are declared but not paid out to you. Instead, they are reinvested at the NAV of the fund after dividend declaration. This results in you receiving more units in the fund and increases your investment capital in that fund. **Expense ratio:** Expense ratios indicate how much the fund charges in terms of percentage annually to manage your investment portfolio. If you invest Rs. 20,000 in a fund that has an expense ratio of 2%, then it means that you need to pay Rs. 400 to the fund house to manage your money.

Exit load: Mutual Fund exit load is a fee charged by the mutual fund houses if investors exit a scheme partially or fully within a certain period from the date of investment, as specified in the Scheme Information Document Different mutual funds houses charge different fees for different schemes as an exit load.

KYC: Know your customer (KYC) compliance is mandatory for investments in the financial markets. To be able to make any investment with a mutual fund house, investors need to ensure that they are KYC compliant with respect to mutual funds.

Management fee: Mutual funds charge management fees to cover their operating costs, such as the cost of hiring and retaining investment advisors who manage funds' investment portfolios and any other management fees not included in the other expenses category.

Management fees are commonly referred to as maintenance fees.

Important terms used in Mutual Fund.

Market risk: Like all securities, mutual funds are subject to market, or systematic, risk. This is because there is no way to predict what will happen in the future or whether a given asset will increase or decrease in value. Because the market cannot be accurately predicted or completely controlled, no investment is risk-free.

Money market: Money market mutual funds (MMMF) are used to manage short-term cash needs. The fund manager invests in high-quality liquid instruments such as treasury bills (T-Bills), repurchase agreements (Repos), commercial papers, and certificates of deposit. Money market funds mainly target earning interest for the unit holders

Mutual funds: A mutual fund is an open-end professionally managed investment fund that pools money from many investors to purchase securities. Mutual funds are often classified by their principal investments as money market funds, bond or fixed-income funds, stock or equity funds, hybrid funds, or others.

NAV: In simple words, the Net Asset Value or NAV is the mutual fund scheme's total value minus the liabilities for every outstanding unit. In no way is the NAV related to the potential of the scheme.

SEBI: A mutual fund is required to be registered with the Securities and Exchange Board of India (SEBI) which regulates securities markets before it can collect funds from the public.

Sponsor: SEBI regulations say that a fund sponsor is any person or any entity that can set up a Mutual Fund to earn money by fund management.

This fund management is done through an associate company that manages the investment of the fund. A sponsor can be seen as the promoter of the associate company.

Important terms used in Mutual Fund.

Redemption: Mutual fund redemption is a process in which you as an investor sell your shares back to the fund Then, as per the needs, the investors may redeem their mutual fund. Also, when the fund is underperforming irrespective of the state of the market the investor may redeem his/her fund.

Switch: Switching in the context of mutual funds refers to the process of shifting your investments from one fund scheme to another within the same mutual fund.

Trigger: Trigger facility is an additional, optional feature provided in mutual fund schemes, which enables investors to book profit automatically at a pre-defined time or value. In other words, the fund declares a dividend, redeems, and/or switches the units automatically on behalf of the investor on the date of the event.

Yield: Mutual fund yield measures the income return of a mutual fund. It is calculated by dividing the annual dividend payment by the value of a mutual fund's shares The mutual fund yield is typically calculated daily with the fund's net asset value (NAV), which is determined after the market closes each day.

Equity fund: Equity funds are those mutual funds that primarily invest in stocks. You invest your money in the fund via SIP or lump sum which then invests it in various equity stocks on your behalf. The consequent gains or losses accrued in the portfolio affect your fund's Net Asset Value (NAV) Debt Fund: A debt fund is a Mutual Fund scheme that invests in fixed income instruments, such as Corporate and Government Bonds, corporate debt securities, and money market instruments, etc. that offer capital appreciation. Debt funds are also referred to as Fixed Income Funds or Bond Funds.

Hybrid fund: Hybrid mutual funds are types of mutual funds that invest in more than one asset class. Most often, they are a combination of Equity and Debt assets, and sometimes they also include Gold or even Real estate. The key philosophies behind hybrid funds are - asset allocation, correlation, and diversification.

Balanced advantage fund: Balanced Advantage Funds, also known as Dynamic Asset Allocation Funds, are a category of Hybrid Mutual Fund Schemes as specified by SEBI that invest in asset classes like Equity and Debt, and keep modifying their asset allocation based on the market valuations.

Overseas fund: International mutual funds are those funds that invest in foreign companies. These funds are also referred to as overseas or foreign funds. Investing in these can be of higher risk exposure, but also chances of higher returns. People usually prefer it as an alternative and (or) long-term investment.

Index Fund: An index fund is a portfolio of stocks or bonds designed to mimic the composition and performance of a financial market index. Index funds have lower expenses and fees than actively managed funds. Index funds follow a passive investment strategy.

Large-cap funds: Funds that invest a larger proportion of their corpus in companies with large market capitalization are called large-cap funds. Large-cap funds are known to offer stable and sustainable returns over a period of time but might be outperformed by small and mid-cap funds, which have higher risk exposure.

Also, according to SEBI, the large-cap, firms have been defined as Firms ranked between 1 and 100 by full market capitalization.

Important terms used in Mutual Fund.

Mid-cap funds: A mid-cap fund is a pooled investment, such as a mutual fund, that focuses on companies with a market capitalization in the middle range of listed stocks. Mid-cap stocks tend to offer investors greater growth potential than large-cap stocks, but with less volatility and risk than small-cap stocks. Also, according to SEBI, the large-cap, firms have been defined as Firms ranked between 101 and 250 by full market capitalization.

Small-cap funds: Small-cap stocks are generally defined as the stock of publicly traded companies that have a market capitalization ranging less than Rs 5,000 crore. ... In a small-cap fund, the fund manager invests at least 65% of the portfolio in small-cap stocks. Also, according to SEBI, the small-cap firms have been defined as Firms ranked above 250 by full market capitalization.

Total return: The Total Return Index (TRI) will give them an accurate picture of a mutual fund scheme before they decide about investing. Right now, all the mutual fund schemes are benchmarked against the Price Return Index (PRI). SEBI found this index as highly inadequate in capturing the holistic performance of a mutual fund scheme.

Investors are advised to understand all the above terms with the help of their advisor or mutual fund distributor before they take the decision to invest their hard-earned money. All successful investors are generally aware of the above terms.

SIP – STP – SWP

SIP (Systematic Investment Plan): Addendums and notices. (SID): A systematic investment plan is an investment vehicle to invest in mutual fund schemes. SIP allow investor to invest a small amount periodically instead of lump sum. The frequency of investment through SIP is usually monthly, quarterly or weekly. Some mutual fund houses allow daily SIP also.

SIP is considered as key to wealth creation. It has many benefits; prime benefit is that you can start with small amount, which could be as low as Rs.100/- per month. It is a tool of wealth creation, if used with starting at an early age, maintaining discipline, investing for a long duration and investing in right asset class.

Following are prime benefits of SIP:

Starting at an early age: One of the advantages to starting early investing is that you have a longer time to invest before reaching the retirement age. It also helps you to accomplish your financial goals by investing in smaller amounts. 5 Reasons to Start Investing Early are: Time allows you to take risks. Typically, when it comes to investing, ventures that are more volatile yield the highest return on investment. Compound interest really makes a difference. Your spending habits will improve. Be a step ahead of everyone else. Your lifestyle will improve.

Disciplined investment: It is a basic law of investing a focus & dedicated towards a financial goal. In a SIP, you have to maintain a monthly balance in your Bank account before it is debited. It is easy to maintain in long run rather than investing a lump sum amount every year.

Power of compounding: As per great scientist Einstein "Power of compounding is the 8th wonder of the world". One of the prime advantages of starting SIP early, since all investments & returns are based on the power of compounding, an investor who starts early can earn much higher returns than those who start late even with a higher SIP amount.

Power of Compounding	Mr. Ram	Mr. Shyam
Starting at age	25 years	35 years
Monthly SIP amount	Rs. 10,000	Rs. 15,000
Assumed rate of return	15% p.a.	15% p.a.
SIP continued till age	55 years	55 years
Total investment	36 Lakh	36 Lakh
Total investment Value	7.01 Cr	2.27 Cr

A difference of almost Rs.5 Cr, is what starting to invest early in life can do to your wealth.

Rupee cost averaging: The SIP method works on the principle of rupee cost averaging. It helps investors to mitigate the timing factor & if you invest regularly, irrespective of the market high or low, it helps you earn higher returns. It is important to know that rupee cost averaging works very well in a long duration. It ensures that you buy more units when prices are low (in a bear market) & you buy fewer units when prices are high (in a bull market) & thereby in the long term your cost of purchase per unit comes down drastically.

Benefit of Rupee Cost Averaging

Month	Price/Unit NAV	SIP Investment		Lumsum Investment	
		Amount Invested	No of Units Allotted	Amount Invested	No of Units Allotted
1	37.50	10000	266.67	90000	2400
2	36.20	10000	276.24		
3	33.80	10000	295.86		
4	31.65	10000	315.96		
5	32.25	10000	310.08		
6	33.85	10000	295.42		
7	35.65	10000	280.50		
8	36.25	10000	275.86		
9	36.85	10000	271.37		
Total Amount Invested		90000		90000	
Average price/Unit		34.89		37.5	
Total no of Units Purchased		2587.96		2400	
Value of investment at the end of 9 Months		95366.3		88440	

Convenience: It is very easy to invest through SIPs becauseit allows investing a small amount every month without any difficulty directly through your Bank account.

Other advantages of SIP:

- The benefit of compounding returns.Can be started with a small amount.
- Can be increased, decrease, paused, stopped, and restarted.
- No need to remember as it is debited directly from Bank a/c on a specific date.
- The benefit of investing in good companies. Professionally managed by highly qualified and experienced fund managers.
- Highly regulated by SEBI, with transparency and liquidity.
- Tax benefit, if invested in tax saver schemes call ELSSunder sec 80C.
- Partial withdrawal or full withdrawal is possible. Few AMC offer life risk cover with SIPs.

There is a saying in English, "Drop by drop makes a mighty ocean". You want a plan that suits you and is financially affordable, more ambitious, and solid, through SIP you can plan for your future dreams. For example, your own retirement planning, kid's education, kid's wedding, etc. Smart recurring a/c is a systematic investment plan, a need for a new generation.

Our forefathers, so far used recurring deposits because of the 11% rate of interest, but now the interest rate is even less than 7% and it is less than the rate of inflation, so now investment through SIP is done in mutual funds to get higher returns and beat the devil known as "inflation".

Type of SIPs:

There are varieties of SIPs introduced besides plain normal SIP by which investment can be done at a fixed or variable or increasing frequency, such as monthly or quarterly.

Top-Up SIP: The first installment is fixed and the incremental amount & frequency of incremental amount is pre-decided, so the investment amount automatically increases at required intervals or once a year. Also known as SIP booster.

Flexi SIP: The first installment is fixed by the investor & subsequent installments are calculated as per a formula to invest more when the market is low & less when the market is high. This SIP is also known as Value Investment Plan (VIP).

Perpetual SIP: There is no end date, however investors has the option to continue SIP till he can and can redeem the amount at a time of their choice.

Multi SIP: This facilitates investing in multiple schemes of a fund house (AMC) through a single cheque & is a great way to build a diversified portfolio in an easy manner.

SIP with free life cover: A bundle of free life insurance cover is provided along with regular disciplined investment by a few mutual fund companies. The insurance is only against the death of the unit holder and is covered under a group life insurance policy by AMC.

SIP or Lump sum investment?

Many investors get confused and could not decide that they shall invest systematically or at one time in a lump sum amount. So they shall consider the following points before deciding on investment:

- SIP is a good idea and ideal for investors who have
- Long-term goals, such as their own retirement or kid's education or wedding.
- Lump-sum investments could also be done for similar goals, however, the value of an investment will keep on varying and will impact the investor as and when the market fall with negative investment value.
- A lump sum investment could catch a higher point in the market; it could also coincidentally catch a low point. So, you gain during lower market points & lose at higher market level.
- SIPs invest regularly, taking away the worry of investing & thereby benefiting from disciplined regular investments.
- SIPs allow you to be benefitted from rupee cost averaging.

STP (Systematic Transfer Plan)

An STP is a plan that allows investors to give consent to a mutual fund house to periodically transfer a certain amount/switch (redeem) certain units from one scheme and invest the same in another scheme of the same mutual fund house.

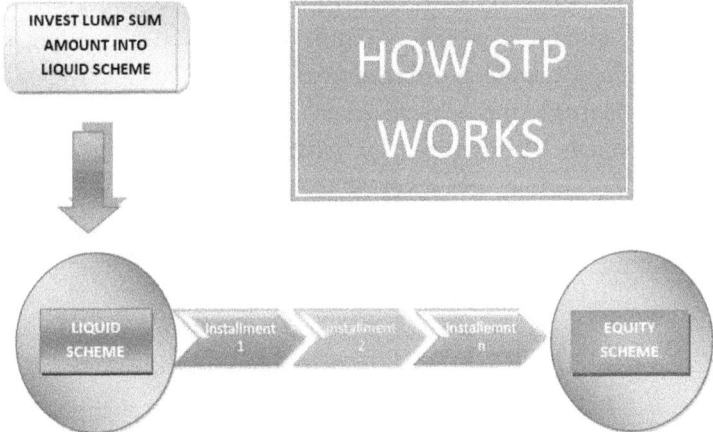

Advantages of STP: The main advantage of STP is the streamlined process of fund transfer & utilization. As the money is automatically adjusted between the selected schemes, an investor can get benefit from the efficient allocation of his available resources. Other advantages are - the power of compounding, rupee cost averaging & disciplined investment just like SIP.

Method: In an STP, an investor invests a lump sum in a fund (usually a debt or liquid scheme) and then transfers a fixed amount regularly to an equity fund. Investors who have surplus money lying idle in their saving bank account can park money in a liquid fund or ultra-short-term fund can do STP to earn a little extra on their lump sum investment.

STP is suitable for investors who are not comfortable investing their money at one time in lump sums in equity funds. STP is also the most suitable method of investing when market-level seems to be high & expected a correction in the near future.

SWP (Systematic Withdrawal Plan): SWP is the opposite of SIP. In SWP investors exercise an option to withdraw a fixed amount of money at regular intervals after investing a lump sum amount in a mutual fund scheme. This withdrawal in a mutual fund scheme act as a steady income for many individuals. For example, for senior citizens. Along with a regular income, the investor may get appreciation on his investment over a long period of time with tax-efficient income.

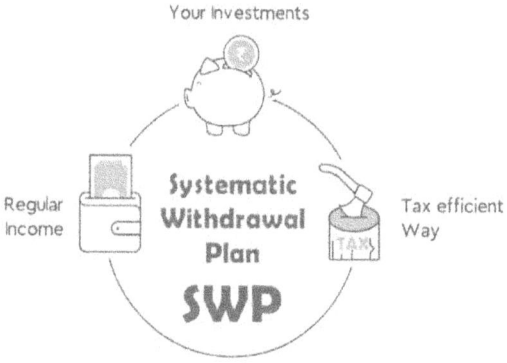

SWP Vs FD:

Fixed deposits with banks are the most popular option for regular income after retirement for senior citizens and retired individuals. But with the rate of interest going down for senior citizens and many individuals SWP option in equity, hybrid equity, or balanced advantage schemes is a good one, who are looking for a regular income with capital appreciation to fight increasing inflation (cost of living).

SIP, STP, AND SWP IN A SNAP SHOT

Parameter	SIP	STP	SWP
Type of Plan	Investment	Transfer	Withdrawal
Process	A fixed amount of money invested in a scheme at regular interval, debited from Bank a/c	The fixed amount of money is transferred from one scheme to another at a regular interval of the same AMC.	The money is withdrawn at a regular interval as per investor's choice.
Purpose	Long term capital appreciation. (Wealth creation for financial goals)	Capital appreciation for excess idle money lying in the Bank a/c.	Capital appreciation and regular tax efficient income.
Taxation	No tax applies to investing. However, capital gain tax is applicable at redemption. i.e. STCG or LTCG	Tax is applicable on every transfer amount as this is considered redemption from the transferee scheme.	Tax is applicable on each SWP amount as it is redemption, there is a cost and a gain tax is paid only on gain amount.
Advantage	Power of compounding, Rupee cost averaging, Disciplined investment approach.	Consistent returns, Portfolio rebalancing, Rupee cost averaging.	Regular income to retired and senior citizens, Offer better benefit than FD or annuities, more tax efficient.

Taxation on Mutual funds: How Mutual Fund is taxed?

Taxation is an important aspect of investment. Every investor must know before investing about tax applicable on their capital gain or on capital loss. There can be a gain or loss on the amount invested by investors. The government may change the tax treatment on investment time to time, so every investor shall get these updates from their advisor or from government publications.

Here we are presenting taxation as per present tax rules, which are subject to any changes by the government in the future, so it shall not be treated as the taxation is permanent or forever. Mutual funds are one of the most popular investment options as they help you achieve your financial goals. Mutual funds are also tax-efficient instruments. Investing in fixed deposits is a great disadvantage, particularly if you fall under the highest income tax bracket, as the interest is added to your taxable income and taxed at your income tax slab rate. This is where mutual funds are the better option. When you invest in a mutual fund, you get the benefit of expert money management and tax-efficient returns.

How do you earn returns in Mutual Funds?

Mutual funds offer returns to investors in two ways:

1. **Dividends:** Dividends are paid out of the profits of the scheme if any. When the schemes are left with surplus cash, they may decide to share the profit with investors in the form of dividends. Investors receive dividends proportional to the number of units held by them.

2. **Capital gains:** A capital gain is the profit realized by investors if the selling price of units held by them is greater than the purchase price. In simple terms, capital

gains are realized due to appreciation in the price of mutual fund units.

Both dividends and capital gains are taxable in the hands of investors of mutual funds.

Taxation on dividends on mutual funds:

As per changes made by the Government in the Union Budget 2020, dividends paid by any mutual fund scheme are taxed in a classical manner. That is, dividends received by investors are added to their taxable income and taxed as per their income tax slab rates.

Previously, dividends were tax-free in the hands of investors as mutual funds schemes use to pay Dividend Distribution Tax(DDT) before making payment of dividends to their investors. During this period, dividends (received from domestic companies) of up to Rs. 10 lakh a year were tax-free. Any dividends in excess of Rs. 10 lakh a year are taxed at 10% asDDT.

Taxation of Capital Gains on sale of units:

The taxation rate of capital gains depends on the holding period and type of mutual fund scheme. The holding period is the duration for which units were held by an investor. It is the time between the date of investment (Purchase of units) and the date of redemption (Sell of units). Capital gains realized only on selling units are categorized as follow:

Fund Type	Shot-Term Capital Gain	Long-Term Capital Gain
Equity Funds	Less than 12 months	12 months and longer
Debt Funds	Less than 36 months	36 months and longer
Hybrid Equity oriented	Less than 12 months	12 months and longer
Hybrid Debt oriented	Less than 36 months	36 months and longer

The short-term and long-term capital gain is taxed at different rates.

Taxation of capital gains of Equity funds:

Equity funds are those schemes whose portfolio exposure of equities is 65% or more. As mentioned above, you will realize short-term capital gains on redeeming your equity units within a year of the holding period. These gains are taxed at a flat rate of 15%, irrespective of your income tax slab rate.

You make long-term capital gains when you sell your equity units if your holding period is more than 12 months. These capital gains of up to Rs. 1 lakh a year is tax-free. Any long-term capital gains over and above Rs. 1 lakh are taxed at a rate of 10%, and there is no benefit of indexation provided.

Taxation of capital gains on Debt funds:

Debt funds are those mutual fund schemes whose portfolio exposure of equity is less than 65% or debt exposure is more than 65%. As mentioned in the table above, you get short-term capital gains on redeeming your debt fund units within a holding period of 3 years. These gains are added to your taxable income and taxed at the investor's tax slab rate.

Long-term capital gains are realized when you sell units of debt fund after a holding period of 3 years. These gains are taxed at a flat rate of 20% after indexation. Also, investors are charged with applicable cess and surcharge on tax. In debt funds, if the holding period is more than 3 years, investors get the benefit of indexation (inflation index) and therefore investor's return is more and tax-efficient.

Taxation on the capital gain of Hybrid Funds:

The rate of taxation on capital gains on Hybrid mutual fund schemes or balanced fund schemes is dependent on the equity exposure of the portfolio of the scheme. If the equity exposure exceeds 65%, then the scheme is taxed like an equity fund, if not then the rules of taxation of debt fund schemes apply.

Therefore, it is very important to know the equity exposure of hybrid fund schemes or balanced funds before investing in them, if not then investors might be surprised by the redemption of units.

The following table shows a summary of the rate of taxation on capital gains on mutual fund schemes:

Fund Type	STCG	LTCG
Equity Funds	15% + cess + surcharge	Up to Rs. 1 lakh a year gain is tax free. Any gain over and above 1 lakh is taxed at 10% +cess + surcharge.
Debt Funds	Taxed at the investor's incometax slab rate.	20% + cess +surcharge.

Hybrid Debt oriented	15% + cess + surcharge	Up to Rs. 1 lakh a year gain is tax free. Any gain over and above 1 lakh is taxed at 10% + cess + surcharge.
Hybrid Equity oriented	Taxed at the investor's incometax slab rate.	20% + cess +surcharge.

Taxation on capital gains when invested through SIPs:

SIPs are a method of investing in mutual fund schemes. They are designed in such a way that investors can invest a small amount periodically. Investors are offered the freedom to choose the frequency of their investment. It can be weekly, monthly, quarterly, biannually, or annually.

You purchase a certain number of units of a scheme through every SIP installment. The redemption of these units is processed on a first-in-first-out basis. Suppose you invest in an equity fund through a SIP for one year, and you decide to redeem your entire investment after 13 months. In this case, the units purchased first through SIP are held for long-term (over 1 year) and you realized LTCG on these units. If the LTCG is less than Rs.1 lakh then you do not have to pay any tax. However, you make STCG on the units purchased through SIP from the second month onwards. These gains are taxed at a flat rate of 15% irrespective of your income tax slab. You will have to pay the applicable cess and surcharge on it.

Securities Transaction Tax (STT):

Apart from the tax on dividends and capital gains, there is another tax called STT. An STT of 0.001% is charged by the government (Finance ministry) when you decide to invest (buy units) or redeem (sale units) of equity or hybrid equity-oriented schemes. For example, if you invest Rs.1,00,000/- the STT will be charged Rs. 1 and your investment amount will be 99,999/-. There is no STT on the sale of units of debt fund schemes.

"The longer you hold on to your mutual fund units, the more tax-efficient they become. The tax on LTCG is comparatively lower than the tax on STCG."

How to deal with Long Term Capital Loss?

As per the provision under Income Tax Act, the Long Term Capital Loss can be set off only against Long Term Capital Gains. Hence, you can set off this loss only against the long-term gain in the previous year. However, if you do not have long-term gains then you can carry forward this capital loss up to 8 years.

Losses on your investments are first used to offset capital gains of the same type. So, short-term losses are first deducted against short-term gains, and long-term losses are deducted against long-term gains. Net losses of either type can then be deducted against the other kind of gain.

According to the tax code, short- and long-term losses must be used first to offset gains of the same type. ... The tax code allows joint filers to apply up to $3,000 a year in capital losses to reduce ordinary income, which is taxed at the same rate as short-term capital gains.

For more details on taxes, we advise consulting a CA or tax consultant while filing IT returns. We advise you to file IT returns every year timely and to show all incomes from all sources to have your finances neat and clean.

Important note: The above tax rates and rules are as per Govt. and it can be changed by Govt. so it shall not be considered for any tax calculations.

Myths and facts about mutual funds.

Myth: Mutual Funds are for Experts.

Fact: In fact, Mutual funds are meant for common investors who may lack the knowledge or skill set to invest in the securities market. Mutual Funds are professionally managed by expert Fund Managers after extensive market research for the benefit of investors. A mutual fund is an inexpensive way for investors to get a full-time professional fund manager to manage their money.

Myth: Mutual Fund investment is only for Long Term. Fact: Mutual funds can be for the short term or for longer-term based on one's investment horizon and objective.

There are different types of mutual fund schemes – which invest in different types of securities – in equity as well as debt securities that are suitable for different investor needs.

In fact, there are various short-term schemes where you can invest for a few days to a few weeks to a few years e.g., Liquid Funds are low duration funds, with portfolio maturity of fewer than 91 days, while Ultra short-Term Bond Funds are low duration funds, with portfolio maturity of less than a year. There are Short-Term Bond Funds which are medium-duration funds where the underlying portfolio maturity ranges from one year – three years. Then, there are Long-Term Income Funds which are medium to long-duration funds with portfolio maturity between 3 and 10 years.

While Equity Schemes are most suitable for the longer-term, debt mutual funds are suitable for investors with short-term (less than 5 years) investment horizons.

Myth: Mutual Fund investing is the same as investing in the stock market / Mutual fund is an Equity product.

Fact: Mutual Funds invest in the stock market (i.e., equities), bond market (corporate bonds as well as govt. bonds), and

Money Market instruments such as Treasury Bills, Commercial Papers, certificates of Deposit, Collateral

Borrowing & Lending Obligation (CBLO), etc. Many of these instruments are not available to retail investors due to the large ticket size of the minimum order quantity (such as G-Secs) and hence, retail investors could participate in such investments through mutual fund schemes.

Myth: Mutual Fund scheme with NAV of Rs.10/- per unit is better than schemes whose NAV is Rs.25/- per unit. Or (A Mutual Fund scheme with lower NAV is better investing in NFO is better than investing in ongoing existing schemes).

Fact: This is a common misconception. A mutual fund's NAV represents the market value of all its underlying investments. **NAV of a fund is irrelevant because it represents the market value of the fund's investments and not the market price.** Any capital appreciation will depend on the price movement of its underlying securities. Let us understand this through an illustration.

Suppose, you invest ₹10,000 each in scheme A whose NAV is ₹20, and scheme B (whose NAV is said ₹100. You will be allotted 500 units of scheme A and 100 units of scheme B. Assuming that both schemes have invested their entire corpus in exactly the same stocks and in the same proportions if the underlying stocks collectively appreciate by 10%, the NAV of the two schemes should also rise by 10%, to ₹22 and ₹110, respectively. Thus, in both scenarios, the value of your investment increases to ₹ 11,000.

Thus, the current NAV of a fund does not have any impact on the returns.

Myth: Mutual funds need a large amount to invest in it.

Fact: Absolutely incorrect. One could start investing mutual funds with just ₹5000 for a lump-sum / one-time investment with no upper limit and ₹1000 towards subsequent/additional subscription in most of the mutual fund schemes. And for Equity-linked Savings Schemes (ELSS), the minimum amountis as low as ₹ 500.

In fact, one could invest via a Systematic Investment Plan (SIP) with as little as ₹500 per month for as long as one wishes to.

Myth: One must have a Demat account to invest in MutualFunds.

Fact: Holding mutual fund Units in Demat mode is absolutely optional, except in respect of Exchange Traded Funds. For all other schemes, including the close-ended listed schemes like Fixed Maturity Plans (FMPs), it is entirely up to the investor whether to hold the units in a Demat mode or in conventional physical accountant statement mode.

Myth: A scheme with higher NAV has reached its peak!

Fact: This is a very common misconception because of the general association of Mutual Funds with shares.

One needs to keep in mind that the NAV of a scheme is nothing but a reflection of the market value of the underlying shares held by the fund on any day. Mutual Funds invest in shares, which may be bought or sold whenever deemed appropriate by the Fund Manager depending on the scheme's investment strategy (Buy-Hold-Sell). If the Fund Manager feels that a particular stock has peaked, he can choose to sell it.

A high NAV does not mean the fund is expensive. In fact, high NAV indicates good performance of the scheme over the years.

Myth: Buying top-rated mutual funds ensure better returns.

Fact: Mutual fund ratings are dynamic and based on the performance of the scheme over time – which in itself is subject to market fluctuations. So, a Mutual fund scheme that may be on top of the rating chart currently, may not necessarily maintain the same rating month after month or at a later date. However, a top-rated fund is a good first step to shortlist a scheme to invest in (although past performance does not necessarily guarantee better returns in the future). Investment in a mutual fund scheme needs to be tracked with respect to the scheme's benchmark to evaluate its performance periodically to decide whether to stay invested or to exit.

Myth: Mutual fund dividends are dividends paid by the underlying stocks in the scheme

Reality – Mutual fund dividends may include dividends paid by the underlying stocks. It also includes the profits made by selling stocks in the scheme portfolio.

Myth: Mutual fund dividends are extra returns over and above capital appreciation

Reality – Mutual fund dividends are not extra returns over and above capital appreciation. Mutual fund dividends are in lieu of capital appreciation.

Myth: Dividend option books profit regularly.

Reality: The underlying portfolio of growth and dividend options of a scheme is the same. Profit booking happens at a scheme level i.e. for both growth and dividend options both. The difference is in how the profits are distributed. In the growth option, the profits are reinvested in the scheme. In the dividend option, the profit or a portion of it may be distributed to the investors at the discretion of the AMC.

Myth: I want to invest in Rs. 10 NAV NFO (NEW FUND OFFER) as they will grow much faster than the existing high NAV fund.

Reality: It is a myth. Someone wants to garner business, nothing else. Mr. A invested in 2008 with a NAV of Rs. 317 and the NAV crossed 2000 after 13 years. Meaning if you would have invested 100000 then it would be 6.3 L after 13 years (15.3% CAGR) There were a lot of MF launched in 2008 with Rs. 10 NAV, and their current NAV was between 50 - 80. Meaning 12 - 18% CAGR. The MF growth depends on their stocks and not depends on NAV.

Financial Freedom – How can you win it?

What is Financial Freedom to you?

- For most people, it is freedom from work.
- Financial freedom is when you can sleep easily with the assurance that all your financial goals will be achieved.
- Financial freedom is not dependent on anyone, Being completely debt-free, having enough money to spend, Having enough money to live without working.

How to win Financial Freedom?

To win financial freedom, one must know that it requires a lot of patience. Financial freedom can't be achieved overnight, in a day or in a year. The process of winning financial freedomtakes a long period of time which can be in years.

Think of a newly born baby, a baby does not grow in a day, in a year but surely he/she takes at least 20 to 25 years to start earning after completion of education. In the same way, winning financial freedom is just like raising a child.

Everybody wants to be free from financial worries but very few people are able to achieve that.

Peoples spend all their working years to earn as much as possible, they do not plan well to get the best. So, despite chasing wealth in their lives, many fail to save enough money to live comfortable life till their post-retirement years. Therefore, to win financial freedom, you must aim for five financial freedoms- from want, from uncertainty, from debt, from loss, and from fraud.

Now we will let you know how to secure freedom from financial worries. From the day you start earning to the day you retire from work; we will cover every step and try to show you how you can adapt planning to keep your hard earn money safe and growing.

Here are 5 ways, if you follow and practice; you can be truly financially free.

FREEDOM FROM WANT:

Put away enough money so that you do not run out of money for your financial goals. Save at least 10% of your income for retirement. Start saving for Kids' education when they are born. Earmark your savings for each specific financial goal. Increase savings in line with rising in your income. Don't dip into savings for discretionary expenses.

The first step in your financial journey towards winning financial freedom is to keep separating your need from wants. From the day you start earning, first, you should save than spend. Many people spend first then save, hence they either do not save or save very little. Save at least 20-25% of your income, which can be 30-40% until you get married. Put at least 10% of your income for your retirement, you may think retirement is far away, but it is closer than you think. Your retirement corpus, when you calculate will be huge and so it is better to think of it first to win with the little amount in long term. You may get a loan and pay EMIs for other financial goals during earning phase of life, but you will not get any loan for your retirement spending in the non-earning phase. We will show you how to make a plan for each financial goal in the next few pages.

What is want and need?

"If you buy things you don't need, you will soon sell things you need"-Warren Buffett.

To win the game of financial freedom and to create wealth over the long run through a systematic and disciplined manner, one needs to know the difference between need and want. Need are those things which everyone requires to live a comfortable life, like food, clothes, a hose, medicine, etc. The wants, on the other hand, are those things which a person wishes he had but they may not be an absolute necessity to have for a comfortable life.

Often people get confused between their needs and wants. A person may need a two-wheeler to reach his office (a need) while he wishes to drive a luxury Car (a want.

FREEDOM FROM UNCERTAINTY:

Don't let unforeseen events and expenses derail your financial planning. Unexpected expenses can destroy even the best financial plan waste. They can set the clock back on your retirement plan and reduce the amount available for a kid's education. To safeguard from any uncertainty in life, buy life insurance that covers 5-6 times your annual income. Buy a health insurance policy of at least 5 lakh for the full family. Keep contingency fund to sustain 6 months' expenses. Take personal accident, disability cover of at least Rs.20 lakh. Insure home and other assets against damage and theft, such as vehicles.

Buy life insurance coverage if you have dependents. The best way to buy life insurance cover with the lowest price(low premium) and highest risk cover (High Sum assured) is to buy a pure term life insurance policy. Term life insurance policy assures you in case of any death of an insured earning member. It does not have any maturity. A 30-year-old can buy term insurance of 1 Cr for only 12000 to 13000 a year.

FREEDOM FROM LOSS:

Don't let greed and fear define your investment planning.

When you invest for your financial goals to achieve financial freedom, your returns on investment come with the risk of being pushed to the bottom. Making risky investments cannot be a good plan. Focus on goals rather than returns. You would be sticking to the principle of not putting all your eggs in one basket. Establish a diversified portfolio and asset allocation. Don't go after extraordinary returns. Rebalance your portfolio at least once a year. Match investment horizon with the asset class. Portfolio asset allocation for example for 40 years of age can be, 60% Equity, 30% Debt, and 10% Gold.

FREEDOM FROM DEBT:

Don't get enslaved by debt due to reckless spending.

Many peoples are careless while spending and borrowing. Credit cards are a spending tool, swiped at will without thinking about repayment. Banks have become active – offering loans, particularly online, with the promise of quick approvals. Landing and borrowing are the prime work of Banks. One should think of repayment before borrowing. Taking a loan is spending your future income at this moment. So, borrowing can be good or bad depending upon repaying capacity of the borrower. Before borrowing and spending one must live within means, differentiating wants from needs. It is easier said than done, as seeing your friend with the latest smartphone, car, or clothes is bound to trigger you to spend. You need to list your needs and wants. Put your best effort to fulfill your needs first then wants. If you must borrow, do not default on repayment. Default on EMI will increase the interest burden and you may be in a debt trap. It will also affect your credit history. That will make it difficult for you to get loans in the future.

Your EMI should not exceed 50% of your income. Do not borrow for luxurious expenses unless you can afford EMIs. Differentiate your wants from your needs. Ensure timely and regular repayment of loans. Do not dip into savings for unnecessary expenses.

CHECK BEFORE YOU BORROW:

Personal loans are very popular, as they are easily available, for personal loans there is no need for any guarantor or collateral security. Before you borrow check about how EMIwill affect your finances. Ask a few questions yourself beforeapplying for a loan.

Is it really necessary to buy now? You might be thinking of buying something but it may not be necessary. Using a credit card for small daily purchases may be fine and can be easily paid before the due date. But using a credit card to buy something you can't afford is not good for your finances. Avoid these unnecessary purchases till you have saved sufficiently.

Can I afford EMI? This is a question that demands an honest answer. Personal loans have a very tight repayment schedule. If you are not sure of paying EMI timely, you should avoid taking a loan.

Should I borrow for a vacation? You may be tired from your job or work and may be thinking of a vacation, but go for it if you have enough cash for expenses. Taking a loan for holiday is not the answer. Vacation is for relaxing from work not for making your life more complicated financially.

When to take personal loans? Personal loans are good for expenses, of 1 lakh or more. These are unsecured loans offered by banks to be used for education fees, medical treatment bills, house improvement, etc. One should find the repayment terms of the loan because they are suitable for 2 or 3 years.

What happens if I can't pay the loan EMI? Before taking any kind of loan, think of the long-term effects. What if you are out of a job in the future? You will face extra pressure to find a job quickly because any late EMI will affect your credit score and you may have a difficult time finding a new job.

To pay interest on something that is unnecessary will most likely turn out to be of low value later is a bad idea. Taking loans for unintelligent reasons or luxuries, helping a friend or relative without a written contract, etc, is a clear path to the financial crisis. So, before taking a loan or helping someone, choose wisely and keep away from seeking a loan just because you can.

FREEDOM FROM FRAUD:

Don't get attracted by the special offerings of high returns on investment by greed.

Avoid investments that offer extraordinary returns. Understand features of insurance policies before purchasing. Adopt safety measures with credit cards, online transactions. Don't fall for fraudulent offers of easy money.

Do not invest blindly in hot stocks or high return schemesbecause your friend is investing in, before investing evaluate investment products on the basis of your risk-taking capacity. In India, there are many Ponzi schemes and fraudulent offers that have wiped out the savings of small investors.

While buying any kind of insurance policies check the purpose and features of the plan, do not buy just because you are convinced by an agent or advisor. You can check online or with insurers. Always question and dig deeper, you have to check and control before making any decision, whether the scheme is regulated by regulators such as RBI, SEBI, IRDA, AMFI, AND PFRDA. Spend time studying the scheme's information or brochure before going ahead.

Make sure you take the pledge to follow towards achieving these five financial freedoms and keep yourself clear of any pitfalls that can put you at risk.

HOW TO WIN FINANCIAL FREEDOM?

Here are 5 steps, if you follow and practice; you can betruly financially free.

- Financial goal setting, positive mindset, cash flow, moneyvalues, enjoy the job.
- Emergency fund, insurances, estate planning. Pay off debt.
- Invest for passive income. Handle your wealth carefully.

To win financial freedom perfect financial planning for each goal is to be done with the assumption of expected return, horizon of goal, rate of inflation, etc. For eg. Every goal can be achieved through SIP investment if you are young, single, or married with kids. You are in the age group of 28 to 35 years. Before you start your SIPs with financial goals, you must have three qualities in your nature, Patience, Discipline a and Consistency, because the equity market is like a roller coaster, when it goes up you enjoy but when it comes downyou are full of fear. SIP returns will not be linear but they willbe with risk and volatility but at the end of SIP journey, yousurely get best results to achieve your financial freedom. So,you need to show strong patience.

Remember that every time fall of the market is replaced withits rise. When there is any fall in the market you may sell your SIP units due to FEAR, which is not a good idea. You cannotcontrol your fear but you can control your ACTIONS to achieve your financial goals. Nobody can predict, "When shall market fall," "How much it will fall", and "How long will ittake to come up". So, it is the best idea to continue SIPs consistently in a disciplined manner even when the market is running low and accumulate more units at a lower cost to achieve your financial goals in a better way. We must not forget and always keep in mind that "Correction is temporary and growth is permanent". After every bear market, one can see a bull market too. Only the period of bear & bull market is not predictable.

5 Steps to win Financial Freedom

What is financial freedom? It's different for everyone, but methodologically, financial freedom is when your passive income (from your own business or assets) exceeds your expenses... allowing you the freedom to achieve your ideal life... and no longer need to work as an employee!

As you finish your degree and enter the professional workforce possibly for the first time, you'll soon realize that a degree, reading the Barefoot Investor and a good pay packet won't be enough to achieve financial freedom. Sure, it's easy to purchase a flashy car these days, but that decision may not put you on a solid path towards financial freedom.

Imagine being able to afford your dream home, live in your ideal suburb, and tick items off your travel bucket list - without having to get out of bed every morning to join the daily work and make small talk around the water cooler with colleagues about your weekend.

Many certified financial planners share 5 simple steps to achieving financial freedom.

5 steps to conquer the financial freedom mountain!

Pyramid diagram (bottom to top):
1. Goal setting, positive mindset, cash flow, money values, enjoy job
2. Estate plans, personal insurances, emergency fund
3. Pay off bad debt
4. Invest for passive income
5. Handle your wealth

Step 1: The Foundations

Clarify your goals, motivations and have a positive mindset that you can achieve financial freedom. Have an automatic cash flow and bank account system that includes a budget to identify your essential expenses, non-essential expenses, and savings plans. Be happy in your job and personal life, as this can help you stay motivated to stick with the plan and reduce non-essential emotional spending.

Financial advice can help with your cash flow, money values, and goals. A psychologist or accredited life coach can help with your mindset and managing your money blocks.

Step 2: Plan B

As your journey towards financial freedom is unlikely to always be smooth sailing, create a safety net to protect you and your loved ones in the event of permanent or temporary illness and disability or premature death. Allocate a portion of your cash savings into an emergency fund of approximately 3 months of expenses (depending on your situation such as whether you have a loan or mortgage).

Personal insurances include income protection, life, total and permanent disability, and trauma insurance that consider previous health issues and cash flow affordability. A financial advisor can assist with your risk management strategy and which products are suitable for you.

Step 3: Going, going gone

Pay off consumer debt such as non-tax deductible high-interest credit cards and car loans. There are various strategies to help pay off this debt sooner. A financial adviser or a financial counselor can advise on the best repayment method for you.

Step 4: Invest for passive income

Investing can be done when you are working for money to provide income later in life when you retire or even when after your retirement.

Investment asset classes generally include cash, fixed interest, shares, and property, with varying growth and income potential. When devising your investment strategy, some things to consider are investment risk, liquidity, investment timeframe, diversification, preservation rules, and tax.

Seeking investment advice from a professional such as a financial planner is a must-do to reduce the risk of inappropriate, costly decisions.

Step 5 – Handle your wealth

Handle your wealth modestly, without overspending or being too generous with your money. Review, monitor, and adjust your investment portfolio when required. Ensure your financial plan remains up to date as your life and goals change over time.

An ongoing relationship with a financial advisor can help.

Financial planning to win Financial Freedom:

Retirement Planning:

Will you have enough for retirement? Find out

As an essential part of your financial wellbeing, retirement planning is crucial. Here's why.

Ideally, the best time to begin planning for retirement is the day you receive your first pay cheque.

When it comes to retirement planning, it requires a proactive approach to plan towards your retirement. The earlier you prepare for retirement; the better will be in the future for you. But no matter where you might be in your retirement planning stage - or how much you need to keep aside for other goals, make a plan that you are financially confident about and stick to it to achieve your retirement goals.

However, before we plan to help you get there, you need to be convinced why retirement planning is crucial for you.

Importance of Retirement Planning

- **Longer life spans:** Today, people, on average, are livinglonger than before. And this can be your very first reason to jump-start your retirement planning. A longer lifespan means more retirement funds to live an easy life when you're no longer working.

- **Anticipate financial obstacles:** It is good to be positive about one's future. But it is also dealing with things sensibly to expect that there may be many hurdles ahead in your life. Therefore, working on your retirement with a strong retirement plan can enable you to overcome any money problems in the future.
- **Leave a legacy:** As a parent, you want to do more for your family. You wish to leave behind an impact that lasts a lifetime and beyond. And to do so, you need to begin today and get your finances in order so that your heirs get benefit from what you sow.

The Right Time to Start Retirement Planning

Ideally, the best time to begin planning for retirement is the day you receive your first pay cheque. So, even though retirement may seem a lifetime away, planning for it in your 20s is not too early.

If you start investing when you are young, you have time on your side to start building good financial habits and benefit from the power of compounding. With every passing year, your investment will generate its own returns - an exceptional wealth-building benefit known as compounding.

Notwithstanding your age, the best time to start saving/investing for retirement is now.

A Guide to Calculate Your Retirement Corpus

Here's how you can create your own personalized financial strategy for your retirement.

Step 1: Understand your monthly expenses

Note down all your monthly expenses at the moment. Make sure you separate out those that will discontinue upon retirement. It is important to note that there are certain expenses that might increase after retirement (like medical) but they can be balanced out by the expenses that might decline (like rentals, clothing, etc).

So, assuming you're a family managed 30, you categorize your family's expenses as follows:

Expenses that will continue after retirement	In Rs.	Expenses that will stop after retirement	In Rs.
Groceries	8,000	Work travelling	5,000
Phone/Mobile Bills	3,500	Home Loan	20,000
Electricity Bill	3000	Child's Education	15,000
Medical Expenses	5,000	Child's Wedding	10,000
Rent	15,000		
Clothing	8,000		
Annual vacation	2,500		
Vehicle Maintenance	3000		
Mediclaim	1,000		
Gifting	1,000		
Total	50,000	Total	50,000

Step 2: Calculate Expected Income after Retirement

If you already expect some income after retirement, based on the various investments you've made in the past years and will continue to make until you're 60.

For the purpose of illustration, let's assume the following amounts in the table below.

From Company	In Rs.
From EPFO	10,000
Pension Policy	10,000
Others	-
Total	20,000

Step 3: Calculate the Net Income Needed After Retirement

Since the expected income from different sources could help you cover some of your monthly expenses after retirement, let's deduct that from your current monthly expenses. Based on our assumptive calculations so far, the present value of net income needed after retirement would be –

Total Current monthly expense	Rs. 50,000
Expected Income	Rs. 20,000
Net income needed	Rs. 30.000

Step 4: Taking Inflation into Account

Now, don't forget that whatever you plan to save for your retirement is likely to be affected by inflation.

So, to understand the buying power of your rupee, you need to look into the future value (after 30 years) of your total expenses by including an assumed inflation rate.

Simply based on the compounding formula, the future value of your 30,000 today will be:

Inflation*	6%
Future Value	Rs. 1,72,304.74

*Inflation is subject to change.

So, the expense will not be the same after 30 years and you need to be ready to meet such high expenses all in the retirement years.

Step 5: Calculate the Retirement Corpus needed at 60

Now assuming that you plan to retire at the age of 60, let's look at the table below that illustrates the total amount that needs to be accumulated on the day you retire, based on 85 years of life expectancy.

Annual Expenses at retirement Age	Rs. 20,67,657
Life expectancy	Rs. 20,000
Cover for how many years	Rs. 30.000
Total Retirement Corpus Needed	Rs. 5,16,91,420.56

So, based on assumptions, we have illustrated that you may require Rs 5.17 crore to sustain your current lifestyle even after retirement.

Where Can You Invest for Your Retirement?

When deciding on an investment avenue, remember to look into your risk appetite and the risks of the investment vehicle. If your retirement is more than 10 years away, you may consider investing in inequities. Equity has the highest potential of earning returns. It carries risks in the short term but that can be eliminated if you stay invested for a long period of time.

You can either choose to make direct equity investments or through Mutual Funds. Direct equity is riskier than mutual funds.

Mutual funds can not only give you exposure to various asset classes and achieve diversification but also help appreciate your investments in the long run with good returns.

A proven way of investing for your retirement is to invest through a Systematic Investment Plan (SIP) in mutual funds. You can begin a monthly SIP that auto-debits your bank account and invests in mutual fund schemes on a pre-determined date every month.

Investing via Systematic Investment Plan:

Is lighter on your wallet.

Provides a disciplined approach towards investing.

Averages the cost of your purchases (Rupee Cost Averaging)through market cycles and volatility.

Offers you the benefit of the power of compounding.

The following illustration may help you understand how investing via a monthly SIP can help you grow your wealth:

Investment Tenure	30 years	30 years	30 years
SIP Amount	Rs. 15,000	Rs. 28,500	Rs. 34,000
CAGR*	12%	12%	12%
Total Amount Invested	Rs. 54,00,000	Rs. 1,02,60,000	Rs. 1,22,40,000
Final Corpus	Rs. 5,29,48,706	Rs. 10,06,02,542	Rs. 12,00,17,068

*The above calculation is only for illustration purposes. The returns will be subject to market trends.

*CAGR: Compounded Annualized Growth Rate.

Along with SIPs, one may also include PPF, NPS, etc which helps in creating a balanced portfolio. You may keep higher allocation into equity-oriented investments in the initial years and reduce equity exposure as you approach the retirement age.

> "And in the end, it's not the years in your life that count. It's the life in your years."
> **- Abraham Lincoln**

How to utilize retirement corpus at 60

The best way to use your retirement corpus is using the SWP method of withdrawal. (Systematic Withdrawal Plan). It is the opposite of SIP. With the help of SIP, you have accumulated a big corpus to be used, when you are no more working.

Now, it's time to use the corpus in a unique way so that you can beat inflation and grow the corpus along with spending for your day-to-day living.

The following illustration may help you understand how you get monthly income through SWP and grow your corpus to leave behind for your heirs.

Retirement Corpus (Invested)	Rs. 5,29,48,706
SWP Period (Yrs)	25 Years (From age 61 to 85)
Growth Rate Assumed	7%
Balance at the age of 85 (Value of Corpus)	Rs. 15,00,00,000
SWP Amount per month	Rs. 1,75,438

As an essential part of your financial wellness, retirement planning is crucial. Taking the help of a financial advisor specializing in retirement planning can help you save the right amount for yourself and your family. They can help you analyze your expenses, prioritize your financial objectives, and show you how to build a portfolio of assets for a fruitful and comfortable retirement.

Begin planning your retirement today and give yourself the ultimate peace of mind. Allow the right financial advisor to help manage your assets and protect you against unexpected losses so that you never got shot in a downswing. Also remember one thing, do not use the investment set aside for retirement for other goals. You should have distinct portfolios for each type of goal.

Kid's future planning example: Assuming you have kid age2 years

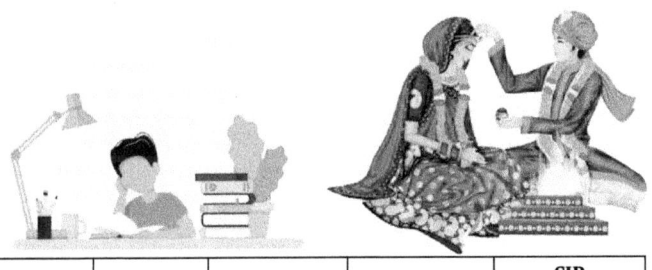

Goal	Goal duration	Current cost	Future cost	SIP required per month
Kid's Education	17	Rs. 20,00,000/-	Rs. 34,000	Rs. 8736/-
Kid's wedding	25	Rs. 15,00,000/-	12%	Rs. 3450/-
	Total	Rs. 35,00,000/-	Rs. 1,22,40,000	Rs.12,186/-

Assumed: Inflation rate @ 5% and Rate of return 12% CAGR.

Above is an example of retirement planning and a kid's future planning, it is just for illustration and cannot be considered as final planning and calculation. Both the above planning and calculation will differ as per age group. In the same way as retirement planning, planning for a kid's education or a kid's wedding can be carried out and can be achieved through SIPs. It will be best in your own interest to take the help of a qualified and experienced advisor to carry out your financial plan to win financial freedom.

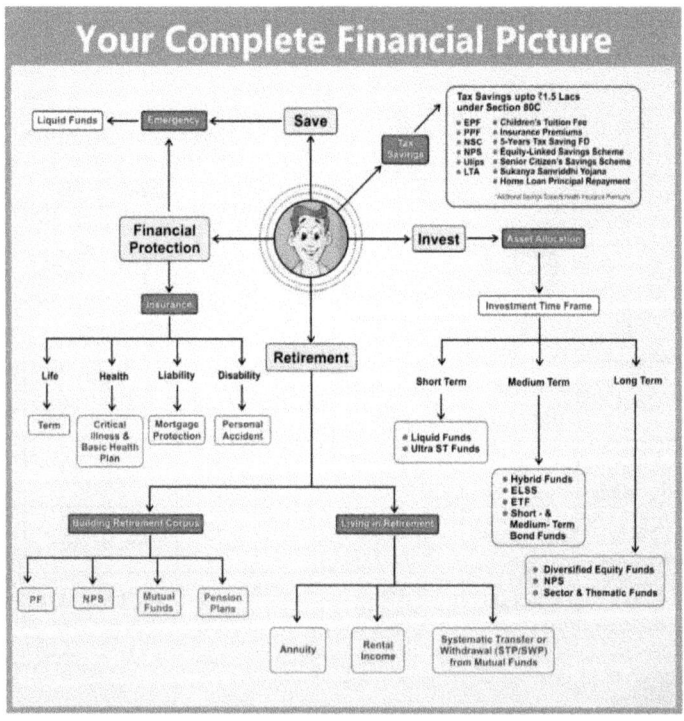

The Role of an advisor!

Who is a financial advisor?

A financial advisor is a person who helps investors in undertaking investment decisions to achieve the desired goal.

There are generally 2 types of financial advisors – mutual fund distributors and registered investment advisors (RIAs). Mutual fund distributors are registered with AMFI and sell mutual fund products to investors. They get a fee from the Asset Management Company and usually do not charge any fee to their customers. RIAs are registered with SEBI who offers investment advice to investors. An RIA may offer a broader basket of products to investors including mutual funds, PMS and other products. RIA charge fee to their customers for the services rendered.

Do you need to have a financial advisor?

If you are an evolved investor and are confident of making the right investment decisions, then you may opt for not having an advisor to handhold or guide you through the investment journey. Mutual funds do offer direct plans wherein an investor can invest without an advisor. However, you should consider several factors when deciding to go direct versus investing through a financial advisor. As mutual funds are subject to market risks, investing in the wrong product can harm your financial interests. You need to make sure that you are investing in the right product that is suitable for your financial needs.

How does having an advisor benefit you?

- A financial advisor will help you with your risk profiling based on your financial situation, financial goals, your age

The Role of an advisor!

- A financial advisor will help you with your risk profiling based on your financial situation, financial goals, your age, and your risk-taking ability. Knowing your risk appetite is important for making the right investment decision.
- Your financial advisor will have knowledge of different mutual fund products, their risk/return characteristics, taxation, and other relevant points. He/she will be able to advise you about the right product for your specific needs. A financial advisor will help you in executing investment transactions like buy, sell (redemption), switches, SIP, SWP, and STP, etc. These transactions can be done either offline (paper-based) or online. If your transactions are mostly offline (paper-based) then investing through a financial advisor can save a lot of time (getting application forms, submitting forms, cheques, and other documents at the AMC or RTA office, etc.).
- You need to be KYC (know your client) compliant to make mutual fund investments. If you are a first-time investor in mutual funds, your financial advisor can help you get your KYC done.
- Patience and discipline are the two most important emotional attributes of successful investors. However, markets can be very volatile making your investment journey bumpy from time to time. Investors often make wrong investment decisions in moments of stress-causing harm to their financial interests. Good financial advisors help their clients remain calm and disciplined in stressful situations.

- Financial advisors can help you track and monitor your portfolio performance and take corrective actions if required.

When should you do a DIY approach?

Direct investing has its benefits in terms of lower cost. However, there is also the risk of making wrong investment decisions in absence of professional advice. Here are some pointers that can help you decide whether you can have a DIY approach:-

- Do you have sufficient experience in investing?
- Do you have sufficient knowledge of different asset classes, mutual fund products, risk profiles, and return potential?
- Do you have knowledge of equity and debt markets? How do they behave in different investment cycles and interest rate environments?
- Can you devote sufficient time to study capital markets and different market indicators on an ongoing basis?
- Can you devote sufficient time to research different mutual fund products, compare different schemes, and select the right scheme based on your specific needs?
- Can you devote sufficient time to monitor your portfolio performance objectively on an ongoing basis? Do you have access to and knowledge of different portfolio performance evaluation tools?
- Are you comfortable carrying out all your transactions online?

You should be honest with yourself when answering these questions. If the answer to all the above questions is yes, then you can invest directly. Otherwise, you should engage with a financial advisor.

What are the qualities to look for in a financial advisor?

Before we discuss the qualities of a good advisor, we will discuss a concern which some investors have. Since mutual fund distributors get commissions on schemes sold to the investor, can he or she sell a wrong scheme just to earn higher commissions? You should know that the regulations are very stringent in this regard. If a Mutual Fund distributor sells a scheme that is not suitable for the investor that would qualify as "mis-spelling" which is an offense and the penalty for the same is very stringent.

Let us now discuss some basic qualities that you should look for in a financial advisor since you have invested your hard-earned money with him/her.

- **Is he/she trustworthy:** Does your financial advisor put your financial interests above any other consideration? It is difficult to judge a person based on limited interaction. You need to have a few meetings with him/her before you start working with your advisor.

- **Is he/she devoting sufficient time to you:** Some investors prefer to work with advisors who have fewer clients, while others prefer advisors who have large practices and many clients. Irrespective of the size of theadvisor's practice and how much you want to invest, your financial advisor should devote sufficient time tounderstanding your needs. Is he/she spending enough time asking you questions about your risk appetite, your investment need, tax situation, etc., or is he/she rushing to close the transaction? Your advisor should schedule regular meetings with you to discuss your portfolio performance / review. If he / she do not do that for whatever reason, then you should take the initiative to schedule the meetings and see his/her response. At the end of the day, it is your hard earned money.

- **How honest and transparent he or she is with you:** If your advisor has made a fund recommendation, has he/she explained why the recommendation is suitable for you in a language that is clear and simple for you to understand? Does he or she schedule regular meetings to review and discuss your portfolio performance? If your portfolio/schemes do not perform up to expectations, does your advisor explain the performance? A portfolio can underperform due to market conditions or wrong decisions. Advisors are also human and can make wrong recommendations. If your advisor is truly honest with you, he/she will admit if they made a wrong recommendation. They will learn from their mistake and make better recommendations in the future.

- **How much your advisor does hand-hold for you:** Different investors need different types of hand-holding depending on their investment experience and knowledge. First-time investors and less experienced investors need more hand-holding. Advisors need to spend more time explaining investment rationale and also guide through troubled waters when the need arises. Even experienced investors may need hand-holding in volatile markets. Bear markets are the true test of financial advisors. Are they responsive to your queries and concerns? A good financial advisor increases engagement in bear markets because this is the time when their clients need them most.

The Role of an advisor!

- **How much he/she works to keep alert about all changes:** Financial advisors are likely to be more informed about developments in capital markets, new products, regulatory and taxation changes, etc. than average investors. Good advisors will be proactive in informing their customers about potential opportunities, risks, or changes so that the investor can make appropriate decisions.

We talked about financial advisors, their roles in helping investors in their financial goals, the pros, and cons of having a financial advisor, and the attributes of good financial advisors. The decision to engage a financial advisor ultimately depends upon the investor. If you think that you can manage your mutual fund investments all by yourself based on the points we have discussed above, you can opt for direct plans. However, in our view, a large percentage of investors in our country, especially new investors, need the services of a financial advisor.

A final piece of advice – you should educate yourself about investments and mutual funds even if you have engaged a financial advisor. We have discussed the attributes of a good financial advisor here, but unless you have sufficient knowledge yourself, you will not know whether your advisor is doing a good job or not.

Wealth creation formulas and moments of inspiration

1. Don't die as poor

I was born in a poor family, a big joint family of my Grandparents, four uncles, four-five aunts, two brothers, and one sister. It was a joint family of 14 members and there wereonly two earning members my father and grandfather. In my childhood, I use to see scarcity of every need. But today my all family members are well settled and financially free. We all have beaten the poverty which took almost one generation. It was possible just due to consistent effort on education and financial literacy.

"If you are born as poor, it is not your mistake, but if you die as a poor, it is your own mistake."

There is no shortcut to being wealthy and rich. To become wealthy and rich one has to go in the line of the process which I would like to mention in this chapter.

"Where the focus goes, Energy flow, Result follows"

In the above slogan, there are only three main words: Focus, Energy, and Result. So it makes a formula:

"Focus + Energy = Result"

It is a practiced and tested formula of my own life. I implemented it in my life from childhood till date and I have achieved desired results too. I got a few results very early and a few results after a few years. Finally, I have achieved financial freedom and I thank God that I was born as poor but will die as rich and wealthy.

Now let us discuss about the above formula of winning over poverty and achieving wealth. Have you realized that in the lives of everyone the Result (achievement) is a product of Focus (Thought) and Energy (Actions)?? Think about it.

For example: You wanted to buy your dream car. For buying a car a thought comes to your mind (it is a focus), now you stats taking actions (flows energy), you check your bank balance for down payments or try to arrange it, you visit a bank for a loan, etc. and after completion of all actions a dream car is bought and it is available in front of your home. (Result or achievement).

So the above formula works knowingly or unknowingly in the life of each and every human being.

I have realized this formula practiced it and implemented it many times in my life and I have achieved desired success and wealth in my life and still using this formula for the betterment of my life and discussed it here for the betterment of the lives of others. Now I hope you have understood the above formula, you too can be successful, rich and wealthy. I hope you too will not die as poor.

Now let us discuss a few more formulas that will help you to be rich, wealthy, and successful in your life.

2. Save and invest before you spent.

Everyone earns money, makes expenses, saves and invests.

The correct formula is

"Income – Saving/investing= Expenses".

Many people spend their hard-earned money immediately after they receive their income from a job or business and due to a devil known as inflation; they either could not save or save a very little amount of money. So it is very important to save first then make expenses.

3. Need and Want.

Everyone wants the best in their life and so they spend on the things they wanted or needed. Here I would like to explain about **want and need**. To become rich and wealthy in life it is very important to know the difference between want and need. If you are smart you will spend your hard-earned money only on your needs and will not spend on your wants.

For example: If your friend or neighbor has bought a very beautiful and costly mobile phone and you saw that brand new successful in any arena, telling them how much you admire them and honor them for their achievements.

The next day you also bought it say on the credit card. Remember you have fulfilled your want. You have not spent your money on your need. Since you had already one cell phone which was good enough to use and was perfectly in good condition, you could have avoided buying the costly Apple phone.

So it is very important to understand your need and want before making any decision of buying anything in the journey of life. In this way, you can save a lot of money, invest a lot of money and make more money from money. Remember the warren buffet's slogan:

"If you buy things you do not need, one day you have to sale things you need."

4. Make money while you sleep.

There are many old age peoples who work for their livelihood even after their retirement. They also started their carrier,earned money but failed to manage their hard-earned money.They did not employ their money to work for them and earn money or money. So it is very important that you earn moneybut let your money also earn money for you and thereby accumulate wealth for your old age expenses. Remember youwill get a loan for buying everything in life but you will never get a loan to buy your retirement expenses. "The best time toplant a tree was 20 years ago, the second-best time is now." **"If you don't find way to make money while you sleep, youwill work until you die". Warren Buffet.**

5. Active and Passive income.

Everyone should know about an active income and a passive income. Everyone is engaged in doing a job, a business, or a profession and by doing so they earn money which is called active income, on the other hand when your money works for you and earns money is called passive income. You invest money and earn a good return on it is also called your passive income. If you have started your earnings from the age of 25 and continued till 55 or 60 (active income), you must start your hard-earned money to make more money by investing in the right asset class. Your invested money must fetch you returns which is higher than the rate of inflation. This way you can have a lot of passive income when you retire from active income.

For being rich it is very important to be in the association of rich people. Read biographies of people who were or are very rich and successful. Use their stories to your own inspiration and learn their success plans. You can read books or attend seminars on investments. You may take courses on how to manage money and grow your money by investing. In this way, you can be more confident when you make your decisions of investing and growing rich step by step.

6. Focus on solutions.

Remember that life is full of problems. Everyone has one or another problem in their life. Only a few peoples fight with their problems and that's why they are very successful but a lot of people fly away from their problems and that's why they are not successful.

In life, each and every problem has a solution. If your focus is only on the problem, the problem gets bigger and bigger but when you focus on solutions the problem looks smaller and smaller. So it is best to focus on the solution rather than the problem. When your focus goes on solutions your mind works to solve them and the problem is solved. By focusing on solutions you take one more step towards being rich, wealthy, and successful.

7. Do not restrict your progress.

In my childhood, my parents and grandparents used to tell me that **"You should spread your legs only as per your bad sheet"** (जितनी चादर हो उतने ही पैर को पसरना चाहिए) but my mentor and my investment gurus taught me that you shall bring the ability to lengthen your bedsheet instead of stoping your legs to spread (पैर को फेलाने के लिए हमे अपनी चादर को लंबी करते रहना चाहते हैं।) I learned a lesson that if you want to spent more or if your expenses are increasing than try to earn moreor more by increasing your ability in which you are good. My elder's advice restricted me from growing on the other had my mentor's advice taught me to break the restriction of growth. I hope readers will find this valuable for their growth too.

8. Equity is equal to business.

At an early age when I was in higher education, I always heard that **investing in the share market is gambling** (शेयर मार्केट में पैसा लगाना जुआ खेलना होता है।) but my investment gurus and my mentor taught me that investing in share market is not gambling it is putting your money into businesses. (शेयर बाजार में निवेश करना कोई जुआ नहीं है, यह आपके पैसे को व्यवसायों में लगा रहा है।)

When I understood that investing in equity is buying a business, before advising others to invest, I started investing my own hard-earned money in 2006 through mutual funds, and today my passive income has increased beating inflation. I am sure that I was born poor but will die as rich and wealthy.

9. An asset and a liability.

In this last paragraph of this chapter, I would like readers of this book also know about two words they are **an asset and a liability.** These two words are very important for being rich and wealthy. These two words will help you and surely will carry you forward in the path of the creation of wealth. You must know the definition and difference between an asset and a liability. You must avoid buying liabilities and you must not avoid buying assets in order to become rich and wealthy. Most people struggle for money their whole life because they don't know the difference between these two powerful words.

"An asset is something that puts money in your pocket and on the other hand a liability is something that takes out money from your pocket."

The rich people buy assets and the poor and middle class buy liabilities. If you are committed to being rich, simply spend your life buying assets. If you spend your life buying liabilities you will never be rich and wealthy.

Let us understand these two powerful words by example. If you buy a brand new car and you are using it for the pleasure of your family and friends, using it for travelling for pleasure then the car is a liability for you because the car is taking out money from your pocket in form of fuel, maintenance, repairs, etc. But the same car is an asset if you are using it as a taxi or a cab or giving it on rent because now the same car is putting money in your pocket and increasing your income.

So whenever you spent your hard-earned money to buy anything in your life think about an asset and a liability before making a decision of buying. Your wise and well-informed decisions will get you on the path of being rich and wealthy.

I wish all those who read this book have a lot of money and become rich and wealthy in their lives by implanting a few formulas which I have mentioned in this chapter and have a lot of passive income so that they all will never die as poor.

Moments of inspiration quotes.

> Successful investing takes time, discipline, and patience. No matter how great the talent or effort, some things just take time: You can't produce a baby in one month by getting nine women pregnant.
> - **Warren Buffett**

- You got to tell your money what to do or it will leave. Dave Ramsey.
- You can avoid buyer remorse by sleeping on big-money decisions. Dave Ramsey.
- Every day is a bank account and time is our currency. No one is rich, no one is poor. We've got 24 hours each. Christopher Rice
- Do not save what is left after spending, but spend what is left after saving. Warren Buffett.
- There are no shortcuts to being debt-free. Get out of debtthe same way you learned to walk – one step at a time. Dave Ramsey.
- I make myself rich by making my wants few. Henry D. Thoreau.
- You are being presented with two choices, Evolve or repeat. Lisa hillier.
- You might get 85 years on this planet. Don't spend 65 years paying off a lifestyle you can't afford.

- If you want to invest in something with minimum risk anda guaranteed big return, invest in yourself.
- Never tell anyone your plans, show them your results. When defeat comes, accept it as a signal that your plan are not sound, rebuild those plans, and set sail once moretoward your coveted goals. Napoleon Hill.
- The only difference between a rich person and a poor person is how they use their time. Robert Kiyosaki.
- Formal education will make you a living. Self-educationwill make you a fortune. Jim Rohn.
- If we command our wealth, we shall be rich and free. If our wealth commands us, we are poor indeed. Edmund Burkelf
- The secret of living well and longer is: eat half, walk double, laugh triple and love without measure. Tiny Buddha proverb.
- The rich don't work for money. They make money workfor them.
- It's not your salary that makes you rich, it's your spendinghabits. Charles A Jaffe.
- You are the root of your financial success or failure. If you work on the root, the "fruits" will take care of themselves.
- If you don't find a way to make money while you sleep,you will work until you die. Warren Buffett.
- The best investment you can make is an investment in yourself… The more you learn, the more you earn. Warren Buffett.

- No matter how great the talent or efforts, some things take time. You can't produce a baby in one month by getting nine women pregnant. Warren Buffett
- I never attempt to make money on the stock market, I buy on the assumption that they could close the market the next day and not reopen it for ten years. Warren Buffett
- Be fearful when others are greedy and greedy when others are fearful.
- Price is what you pay, value is what you get. Warren Buffett
- Look 3 things in a person. Intelligence, Energy & Integrity. If they don't have the last one, don't even bother with the first two. Warren Buffett.

Book reviews by industry experts.

Thanks to increasing financial awareness, more and more savers are turning to investors. Such investors will find this book hugely beneficial to start their financial journey on a sound footing. Most of their queries are answered here in lucid and friendly language. Existing investors will also get value and insight from this book as it covers important topics such as asset allocation and financial freedom in detail. Mr. Patel shared with us his understanding and experience that he had garnered over 20 years while witnessing many changes in the industry and market events firsthand. Wish this book to be read by maximum investors and looking forward to more such enlightenment from him in the future.

Shirish Patel – Prudent CAS (CEO)

To earn money is one thing while saving, investing, and growing your money is totally different thing. The art of growing money is the solution to almost all your questions about how to grow your money so that you can achieve and enjoy your financial freedom. Managing and investing money is a very complex subject. Mr. Chhabilesh Patel has simplified this subject very level in this book. They say, books are our best friend, and I strongly believe this book has all the qualities of a best friend. A true friend helps and guides you throughout your life. Art of Growing money will also guide be your lifelong companion and will guide you on all your financial decisions.

Jigar Parekh – Anchor EDGE (Founder & CEO)

Book is amazing to understand the basics of investment insimple language

You can learn why to invest, how to invest and where to invest based on your goal along with Taxation.

Must read once and clear your concept of MF.

Chirag Modi – Prudent CAS (Zonal Manager)

The concepts of this book are very easy to understand, the author has told the most complex things about money with so much ease and simplicity that even a 10-year-old child can understand it. I personally recommend all new as well as existing investors to read this book to update themselves.

Priyank Thakkar - Prudent CAS (Area Manager)

I know Chhabilesh Patel since about 2006 when I first met him for Mutual Fund. He then done his own investment in MF and then told his relatives and Clint. He has never considered his own benefits and has always looked after the interest of the investor. Chhabilesh Patel takes care of the smallest details of all his investors and also keeps a record of documents and investments. He is a very gentleman, he has served his parents very well, he has brought up his both children very well, which proves his gentleness. If we talk about the book written by him, this book proves his mastery in the field of his thoughts and investment. It is very simple and well described for mutual fund investors. Every investor should read this book at least once in a while.

Ayaz Mansuri – Prudent CAS (Cluster Manager)

This book is one of the best book for young age people who wants to know about the basics of investments... I love the topic of savings vs investments and the way they elaborate.. Nowadays it is very important to understand the value of investment because the only thing which beats inflation is the equity or mutual funds...

Thank you Chhabilesh Bhai for the wonderful book.

Krunal Kansara (Senior Manager)ICICI Pru Mutual fund

Take Action!! Take Decision!!

We all are blessed by God with a mind and time. It is up to you how to use them. With each Rupee when it comes in your hand, it is up to you how to use it. Only you have the power to decide your own destiny. Spend your money foolishly, spend it on liabilities or invest it to learn how to create assets. If you are deciding to buy assets you will be rich & achieve your financial goals & achieve your bright future. The choice is yours & only yours. Each & every day with every Rupee, you decide to be rich or poor.

Even in Bhagvat Geeta Lord Krishna has told us to take good actions and decisions, and don't think of results, the results are the product of our decisions & actions.

Thank you for reading this book, you can choose to share this invaluable knowledge with your children and you prepare them for their good future. No one else will. You determine your future and children's future by your own actions and decisions, you make today, not tomorrow.

I wish you and all the readers of this book great wealth, happiness, and prosperity in their life.

Chhabilesh Patel. MFD

Soham CapiGrow

This book will provide many insights to not those who are just new to mutual fund investments but also to those who are investing in the mutual fund for a long period of time.

Mobile no. +91 9638394693

Email id : sohamcapigrow@gmail.com Website: www.sohamcaapigrow.com

Copyright @CHHABILESH PATEL Published By: SOHAM CAPIGROW Let your money earn…